THE DIARY OF
JINKY

Dog of a *Hollywood* Wife

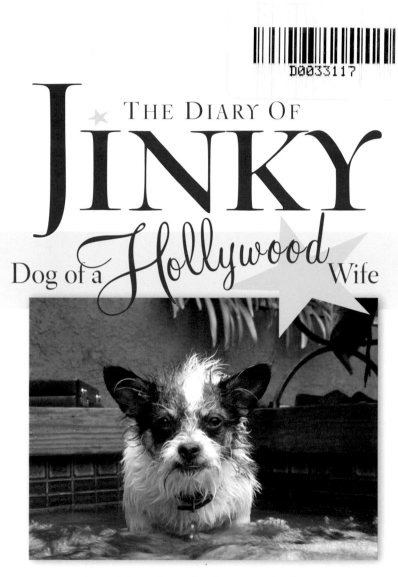

As told to Carole Raphaelle Davis

**Andrews McMeel
Publishing, LLC**

Kansas City

06 07 08 09 10 SDB 10 9 8 7 6 5 4 3 2 1

ISBN-13: 978-0-7407-6048-8
ISBN-10: 0-7407-6048-3

Library of Congress Control Number: 2006923124

www.andrewsmcmeel.com

Book design by Diane Marsh

To my husband,

KEVIN ROONEY,

the funniest man in Hollywood,

and to

KIMI PECK and JANET WINGFIELD,

for rescuing Jinky

ACKNOWLEDGMENTS

J'd like to thank Shelley and Mark Brazill for their help in making this book possible. Many thanks to Bill Brazill, Ritch Shydner, and my agent, Aviva Layton.

Special thanks to Hal Moore, Supervisor of San Pedro Animal Control, who made the call that saved Jinky's life.

Dorothy O'Brien and Andrews McMeel, thank you for bringing Jinky's story to the public. Teri Austin of the Amanda Foundation deserves my heartfelt thanks for all of her hard work helping animals, for rescuing Zelda, and for teaching me so much about the issues. I am grateful for Elaine Seamans, who rescued Finley.

Chris DeRose, founder of Last Chance for Animals, is a true American hero who has gone to war on animal cruelty. He has taught me what I never wanted to face and what I can do to help change it.

I thank Karen Dawn of Dawnwatch.com for her efforts to bring us the news we need in order to effect change.

Thank you, Chihuahua Rescue, for saving Jinky's life and thousands of other lives. And thank you to all the kind people who take action on behalf of animals, who work, give, struggle, and strive to make humanity more humane.

INTRODUCTION

My life began in a cage in San Pedro, California. Some creepy guy bought me for his stupid wife and she didn't want me. I stayed in their dirty concrete apartment for a couple of months while they smacked me around. Then one night, the guy took me to the pound. They threw me into a cold, wet crate and slammed the gate. It was the most horrible place—they call it a shelter but it was more like a death factory. I knew what was going on there; I saw the dogs getting dragged out of their cages. They'd get a noose put around their neck and get pulled down the hall, pissing themselves. Then I'd never see them again.

I was scheduled to be "put down" or, as I like to say, murdered. But I got lucky. The night I was supposed to be killed, a really nice lady named Janet took me out of there and drove me to Burbank, where I ended up in Chihuahua Rescue. I don't know how they thought I was a Chihuahua, because I'm not, but hey—I wasn't going to complain. I was getting two squares and a warm blanket.

That weekend, they brought me and about fifty other dogs to an adoption day at a pet store in Burbank. A lot of oddballs were walking around looking for a cheap dog. Lucky for me, my mom and dad were two of them. I didn't know it then but he's always looking for a cheap way to do something, and my mom refuses to buy a dog on moral grounds and would only adopt.

So anyway, my dad saw me in my cage and called my mom over. "Look at this crazy-looking little guy! Looks like a fruit bat!" They took me out of the cage. I was on my best behavior. They even had a cute blond Cairn terrier girl named Finley with them.

They took me up to their house to see if I could get along with her and the cat they had up there. Right away, I knew I had hit the big time. Their place was amazing. And they were *nice* to me. It was the first time in my life that anyone had *ever* been nice to me.

To think that I was on death row in San Pedro and now I've got a house in the Hollywood Hills with a pool, sports cars, a hot blond girlfriend—she's fixed and I've got no balls; we're the complete Hollywood couple! I've got it made. I've even got a mom and dad who love me. I'm really happy. The funny thing is, they're *not.*

All my mom and dad do is complain. My mom used to be somebody, but she doesn't want to remember who that was. She started as an underwear model. She made records, and she was in movies and on TV. Now she just lounges around in her underwear for no pay. My dad is a writer—or at least he sleeps at the computer a lot. My mom complains about not making any money and my dad makes plenty of money and complains about spending it. Turns out, they're typical show biz people. They're impossible. And Mom and Dad are just the tip of the iceberg. Their friends are all nuttier than they are.

But, that's Hollywood—a lot of neurotic people and lucky dogs.

The Perfect Poop

Last night there was a mysterious poop on the bed.

It was beautifully proportioned, shaped like a Tootsie Roll.

Mom smelled it when they came back from a party but couldn't tell if it was real or just a bad fart. Dad was groping around the bed for his glasses, like he always does, and he grabbed the perfect poop instead.

Dad: "Arg! It's a piece of shit!"

Mom: (laughing) "Who would poop on the bed?"

Dad: "Well, it wasn't me."

Then Dad got all mad about the duvet cover.

Dad: "I can't see anything on this goddamned black paisley duvet cover. How much did this goddamned thing cost, anyway?"

Mom: "Do you have to yell and swear?"

Dad: "Yes, I have to yell and swear. I was looking for my glasses and got a handful of shit instead!"

Mom: "Your glasses are on your head."

Dad: "I don't care where they are, I still got a handful of shit! Why do we have a black bedspread?"

3

Mom: "Because it's pretty."

Dad: "Who *cares* what it looks like? We're asleep under it! Why can't we have plain white sheets like normal people?"

Mom: "I suppose I could put the white sheets on so we can spot the shits in the bed more easily."

Dad: "Right. Let's not *not* shit in the bed, let's have white sheets so we can spot the shits in the bed more easily. *That's* the solution."

They have no idea whose poop it was.

After Dad got a Kleenex and flushed the perfect poop down the toilet, he came back to bed and stepped right on *another* piece of poop that had fallen on the floor. It was all part of the same perfect poop and Dad had to go back into the bathroom to clean it from between his toes.

Dad: "Jesus! I'm gonna fall asleep and roll over and get a mouthful of shit in the middle of the night here! We better check the rest of the bed."

Mom: "Oh my God! There's another piece! Look at it!"

At the end of the bed, on the 800 thread-count black duvet cover, camouflaged in the print, lay the tail end of the perfect poop. It was tapered like a little *cornichon*, those expensive French pickles Mom serves at dinner parties.

Dad gave a big sigh, walked really slowly to the

bathroom, got a piece of toilet paper, and threw away the last of the perfect poop.

The perfect poop didn't stop them from that crazy naked wrestling they do. Mom might have gotten hurt so I tried to get in between them but it was over really fast and they looked pretty happy.

Guess Who's Not Coming to Dinner?

Mom and Dad are having another dinner party and they invited a bunch of music and TV people. They spent hours putting it together and making all these calls and then they left us here in the house alone to go food shopping.

While they were out, the phone rang a lot more than usual, so I went into the den to listen to the answering machine. What a joke.

The guests all started canceling like they always do. They gave bullshit excuses like, "We have a house inspection tomorrow and we're refinancing," or "I'm on a deadline for CBS, they need the script by morning," or "I hate to do this so last minute, but I have to go to a birthday party." Really they've just got better parties to go to with people who are more important than my parents.

I'm glad their party fell apart. I won't have to try not to bite people who pretend to like me and we can just be all cozy in a pack in front of the fire.

When Mom and Dad came back and got the messages, they blew up.

Dad: "I'm out of the business!"

Mom: "I'm going to give all this fish to the cat!"

Why did they have to buy fish? (We always end up with fish at parties because Mom won't eat meat and

Dad hates vegetables. That equals fish.) The cat doesn't do anything useful around here and now she's getting a $70 meal.

Evil Terriers

We got presents for Christmas! We got stuffed toy monkeys that scream! The monkeys scream this ear-piercing call when you bite them and Finley kills them fast. She bites down hard and cracks the spine. She's an evil terrier and she kills for fun.

Mom thinks she's an animal rights activist (she's really a cheating vegan) and she yells at Finley about her killing instinct, but she can't help it. Finley won't sleep until her monkey is dead.

I'll tell you one thing, I keep the noise level down around Finley.

My Arranged Marriage

Not all arranged marriages are happy but mine is. I love my wife, Finley. She's stubborn, willful, delinquent, fickle, greedy, and unapologetically lazy, like most wives.

She's my big, sexy, dumb blonde. I love her so much I can hardly look at her sometimes because I get too emotional and also because I have no balls.

Action Star Dog

We went down to West Hollywood yesterday and ran into an old friend of Mom's who told us the craziest story.

There's this guy who's been loitering around Hollywood for dog ages trying to get a movie sold. He was hanging around the Sky Bar on Sunset Boulevard when he finally met a major Hollywood action star who invited him up to his house to pitch a movie.

The guy drove up to the house and rang the doorbell; Action Star opened the door and invited the guy in. As soon as the guy stepped in the door, the action star's rottweiler took a big bite out of the guy's winky and balls.

The bite must have been pretty bad because the guy was rushed to a lawyer and then to the hospital.

His big break became a big *bite*. When he was invited up for lunch, he didn't think he'd *be* lunch.

It's a lot harder to be a writer than I thought. Dad goes to a lot of pitch meetings. I hope it doesn't happen to him.

Yogaphony

Mom almost strangled a mop today. She was mopping the floor when the phone rang. It was that Yogaphony calling. I heard the whole stupid conversation on speaker phone.

Yogaphony: "Hi! How *are* you?"

   Mom was about to tell her how she was when Yogaphony cut her off.

Yogaphony: "Is Kevin there?"

Mom: "He's at work right now."

Yogaphony: "There is something I want to talk to him about. I've got this new yoga video . . . oh, I just realized! You would have been so perfect for it!"

Mom: "You should have called me."

Yogaphony: "Next time I will."

   Mom started wringing the mop head really tightly and then shaking it and banging it in the sink.

Yogaphony: "I've got this new yoga video, ya know, and I'd like Kevin to introduce me to Jay Leno. I know he's a friend of his and anyway,

I thought it might be good for Jay to do some funny yoga positions on *The Tonight Show* in a leotard and I could show him some of my moves and plug my new video."

These Hollywood people never stop plugging, pushing, and clawing to appear on TV.

Mom: "Well, I'll be sure to give him the message that you called. Whose house are you living in right now so he can return your call?"

Mom always cleans best when she's angry. You could eat off the kitchen floor, which we do, by the way.

Wigged Out

Mom and Dad went to a wig party wearing cheap wigs. Mom's got a long platinum blond wig and she looks like an old stripper. Dad looks like a drugged-out rock star from the '80s. I love them but, really, what a pathetic duo.

This is what I had to look at last night.

Ever since Mom and Dad were invited to that wig party, they've been behaving strangely. Dad has been bald since he was twenty-three and now he thinks he looks good in his hair hat.

Dad: "I could have had a whole other life if I had had hair! I could have been a leading man."

I'm worried about Dad. He spends hours staring at himself in the bathroom mirror.

Dad: "I'm going to move to Paris and just wear hair. I'll invent a whole new persona and be an aging Irish rock star. . . . No one will know I'm bald! We'll go to museums and restaurants and I'll have . . . *hair.*"

Mom can't stop laughing, but I can tell she's looking at him in his hair and getting all hot over the idea of him as an Irish rock star.

Mom: "You should just start wearing it on the plane on the way to France and start a whole new life over there."

Dad: "It kinda makes my body look different, doesn't it?"

Mom: (cooing) "It *does*. Your head looks so much *bigger.*"

Dad: "First thing in the morning, I'm going to renew my gym membership. I'm gonna work *out.*"

Dad was getting excited looking at Mom in *her* wig. And then I had to witness the grossest thing I ever saw: my parents doing that crazy naked wrestling thing they do, only this time in wigs, pretending that they were wrestling with complete strangers. I don't get it. I *bite* strangers.

I did my best to stay out of their way, but they were all over the bed. Even Zelda, who never reacts to anything, walked out in protest. Finley slept through the whole embarrassing thing. I tried to hide under the shams until it was all over. Thank God it was only a few minutes.

Journey to the Bottom of the Pool

Mom made a delicious Pasta Puttanesca last night for me, Dad, and her old friend Corinne, who was a "Pet of the Year." She didn't look like a pet, she wasn't furry or anything. She looked like she had giant pillows on her chest—big dog beds that looked cozy.

Mom was going on and on about Puttanesca sauce instead of giving me a bowl of it.

Mom: "It's called Puttanesca sauce, after puttana, meaning *whore* in Italian. They used to make it in the brothels in Naples. . . . They thought if it was really spicy hot, it would kill venereal diseases."

The Pet reached down and gave me some. While I was slurping up a particularly long spaghetti with sauce and Parmesan, Dad's chair broke, dropping him to the floor, under the table. *Blam*! He got all red and screamed.

Dad: "Aaaaaaaargh! Goddamnit! Aaaaaaaaaaaaaargh! Why? Why! Why—aaaaaargh!"

Then, he picked up the chair, opened the door to the balcony, and hurled the dinner chair over the balcony down into the pool. Every time something goes wrong, Dad throws something into the pool. You think you can find a lot of good stuff in the wreck of the *Titanic*? You should dive down to the bottom of our pool sometime.

Mom: "Don't throw the chair in the pool *please*! Don't
     start throwing things around, you're scaring the
     dogs!"

I wasn't scared, I was eating that Italian whore
sauce. Dad would never throw us in the pool.

Mom's Pet friend was laughing so hard, she was
dabbing her eyes with her napkin and making squealing
noises like a squeaky toy while Dad stumbled in his
clogs on his way back into the dining room.

Then, Dad took off his shoes, growled like a wild
beast, and threw his clogs way out past the pool and
into my poop area, down the mountain, under the
Hollywood sign.

After dinner, Mom, her old Pet friend, and Dad
settled in the library to look at some châteaux
for sale in Normandy on the Internet. What idiots.
They're never happy with what they've got. I never
dreamed of having a pool and a big yard when I was on
death row in San Pedro.

It was not a great sleepy night. They took piles
of papers down to the bedroom and watched the opening
bell of the London market on TV, really loud.

Then Dad called London and made maneuvers with his
euros. They put him on hold.

Dad: "I gotta stop the bleeding! I feel like a sit-
     ting duck here with these idiot brokers! The euro
     could go into a free fall! Don't these idiots
     know that the Forex Desk is open in London? I'm
     going to have to teach them how to do their job!"

I wish Dad didn't get so mad about his euros
going up and down. I mean, all we need is a bed and

some food. I think Mom and Dad are obsessed with all the wrong things. All we really need is to be in a pack. It doesn't matter where. We could always make do in a cave somewhere.

Dad got tired of waiting on hold.

Dad: (yelling) "How long are these idiots going to keep me on hold? Goddamnit!"

Dad got up, threw open the bedroom door, went out on the balcony, and threw the phone into the pool.

Mom: "You're insane."

Dad: "I'm insane, and they're on hold . . . AT THE BOTTOM OF THE POOL!"

Ant-y Maim

Dad came out of the bathroom last night batting his head with both hands.

Dad: "Jesus! I have ants crawling all over my head! I've always got ants on my head. I keep finding them around the back of my ears!"

Mom: "Lemme see. There's nothing on your head but freckles. Nothing. Not a hair, not an ant, nothing. But I know what I'm going to give you for Valentine's Day: an ant farm."

They are so sick. On Monday, they are going to the lawyer's office to change Dad's will because it hasn't been amended since Mom and Dad were married. This has led to some very interesting conversations.

Mom: "What if I get breast cancer, lose my tits, and get lesions on my brain? You know, there's a new study out that says if I have migraines I might have lesions on the brain. What if I lose my tits and my mind?"

Dad: "If you lose your mind and you still have your tits, you'll be OK. I'll keep you and wheel you around in a chair. But if you lose your tits, that's it! You're out. You'll have to scavenge around for bread somewhere under a bridge. I'm not going to spend the rest of my life with a titless smart-ass."

Mom and Dad worry about so many things that haven't even happened. That's where people are dumber than dogs. I like a good nap, a good meal, a little bake in the sun. If they had one night, just *one night*, on death row, they might realize they're happy right now . . . like me. If only they had tails they could wag.

Sleepless in Paris

I've been busy flying back and forth to France because Mom and Dad don't feel like such losers overseas. I haven't felt like a loser since I got out of the pound. I wish the people who beat me up and dumped me in the pound could see me now—I'm in Paris!

That gold dome over there is where some dude named Napoleon was buried. I hear he died with pug bites

all over his body because his wife, Empress Josephine, had ten pugs in her bed and the pugs wouldn't let Napoleon in the bed. He was supposedly a real badass who conquered the world but he couldn't get past a platoon of pugs.

I guess we make it hard on Dad in the bed, too. Last night Finley moved beds at least five times. She ended up in the big-people bed (Duxiana—thousands of springs), pinning Dad down by sprawling out over the comforter. He couldn't move and just laid there with his eyes open.

I had a flea crawling around my ass for hours and I couldn't reach it, so I guess I kept Dad up with my scratching.

Dad: "I'm going to kill myself. It's the only way I'm ever going to get any sleep."

Pinning Dad so he can't move during the night

Homeland Insecurity

Mom and Dad are seriously considering convert-
ing everything to euros. They talk a lot about a day
of reckoning for the dollar. Today, my squeaky ball
costs 37 percent more U.S. dollars than it did a
year ago.

It's pretty scary to think that the value of my
yard and Finley's rat-hunting areas will collapse
with the implosion of the housing market and the
radical devaluation of the dollar.

I'm worried that the Department of Homeland Security is going to make it impossible for us to go to Europe. What if they start searching us and weighing us? What if our travel bags aren't accepted anymore? Already, starting in June, we have to have new rabies exams, more detailed testing, and we have to have international chips put under our skin. Like *dogs* are the problem. What are they looking for, a fuse coming out of my butt?

Back in Loserland

The Emmys are on tonight and Dad is grumpy. He won't let Mom have an Emmy party.

Mom: "I don't see why we can't have people over that hate all the same people we do!"

Dad: "I have things to do. I'm going to go downstairs and get my computer going. You do whatever you want."

Dad got a fancy Mac laptop over six months ago and still hasn't powered it on because he can't figure out how to get online. He says he's just going to use a typewriter.

Dad: "Anything that is any good was written on a typewriter, not on these goddamned machines. I can't get the thing to work! I've spent thousands of dollars, thousands! Nothing works like a book, a bicycle, and a library card. I'm gonna sell everything and go live in a van."

Mom: (sighing) "Here we go."

I don't know why Dad is being such a grump about the Emmys. He has two Emmys. I think he might throw the unused laptop in the pool, like he did with the last one.

Dad not wanting to watch the Emmys is like me not wanting to watch the Westminster Dog Show. It's ridiculous. I like to watch the hot bitches. I don't feel like I have to win or that I should be there, kissing the ass of some fat-calved "handler" for a crappy dog food endorsement.

"We're in a LOSER DEATH CLUTCH"

Sleeping with the Emminy

Right after we watched the Emmys last night we went to "the Down" (the bedroom downstairs) and watched Mom have a tantrum about not finding her 800 thread-count pillowcase.

She had just taken the gigantic sheets out of the dryer and was struggling with them, yelling and whipping them in the air like boat sails.

Mom: "How can I lose a pillowcase between the bedroom and the laundry room? *Where is it*?!"

Dad was depressed about the Emmys and picking his face in the 10x magnifying mirror in the bathroom.

Mom: "Can't you *help* me find the pillowcase!?"

Dad came out of the bathroom with a red nose from all the picking.

Dad: "Jesus! I don't give a shit about the pillowcase. Do we have to find it tonight? Don't worry about it."

Mom: "That's what you say about *everything* in this house—'don't worry about it'—and that's why everything is so *disorganized*!"

Finn and I were trying to find a cozy spot in the bed but Mom kept ripping all the sheets off, looking for the pillowcase, so we couldn't get cozy at all. We just sat on the floor. Then Mom found the pillowcase inside another pillowcase.

Mom: (sheepishly) "I double bagged. I put a pillowcase on a pillow and then put another pillowcase on top of that."

Finally, she made the bed and we were able to get comfy on the comforter. Mom and Dad both got into their spots and Dad pulled the covers way up over his head.

Dad: "I'm all pimply. I'm a pimply old man."

Mom: "What's wrong with you *now*?"

Dad: "I can't believe that dumb show won an Emmy."

Mom: "Would you *stop*? What do you care about who wins Emmys?"

Dad: "An Emmy is a chocolate-covered banana for the monkeys who run the networks."

Mom: "You have two! You want *another* one?"

Dad: "Mine are ten years old. Old and useless, like a ten-year-old banana."

Mom: "You're still an Emmy Award—winning writer."

Dad: "An old, pimply, Emmy-winning writer. I'm going to go to a pitch meeting tomorrow with a face full of pimples. Why would a network give a show to a man who has a face full of pimples?"

Mom: "Pimples are good! They'll think you're a teenager!"

Dad: "A *bald* teeneager!"

I was trying to sleep but Stupid Kitty started scratching around in her litter box again. She makes a hell of a lot of noise, pawing away at those stinking "pearls" that absorb all of her superpungent pee. She scrapes the "pearls" from one side of the stinking box to the other side, and then does it again— for *cleanliness*. She really does stink up the entire Down. Even though Stupid Kitty's litter box is in the laundry room, it's still only a feeble ball-toss away from the bed.

Honestly, I don't know why Mom has Stupid Kitty's bathroom right in front of the dryer, where the clean sheets come out. I'd rather have fleas in the sheets than those pungent piss pearls.

I went to sleep to the sound of Mom and Dad talking. It doesn't matter what they say—it's soothing.

Dad: "I'm a loser."

Mom: "If *you're* a loser, what does that make me?"

Dad: "You're a loser too. Even the dogs are losers. We had to get them out of the garbage. They were thrown away before we got them. We're all stuck in a loser death clutch."

Then Mom and Dad laughed like hyenas. I don't ever think I've seen them laugh so hard. They are truly crazy, those two.

Gasbags in Paradise

Dad had a big meeting here at the house. What a bunch of gasbags. Dad and *Last Comic Standing*'s Gary Gulman are trying to get a series on the air about a neurotic relationship between a "Peter Pan" guy and a "likable" woman (likable meaning *unlike* my mom). We were forced to stay up way past "Minky Time" (10:00 p.m.) so that "actors" and "producers" and "managers" could posture around our dining room table and come up with a decent story to pitch to NBC tomorrow.

The million-dollar dog bed that Dad doesn't like to sit on because it makes him feel like Euro-trash

No one gave me any food.

Dad and Gary Gulman are going to pose as a "hit-making dynamic duo" so that the NBC minions won't be able to pass on their show.

Manager: "These guys will win back the cable audience
for network TV!"

I guess I'm supposed to be impressed that a big star is sitting next to me. Gary Gulman's head almost reached the lights in the ceiling. He's taller than a borzoi! But he didn't give me anything! No Brie, no candied dates with mascarpone cheese, no Brazil nuts, not even a look. Nothing.

While I tried to sleep, Gary Gulman, the comedic genius who ignored me for about five hours straight, told a story about how he doesn't want to tell his mother about his girlfriend yet. They've been going out for four years.

Mom looked shocked.

Then the *Last Comic Standing* heartthrob sat on *my* giant dog bed, eating dates. No "thank you," not a pat on the head, nothing. And then he marked the bathroom! I don't know how I will pee on top of his pee, he's so tall.

Listen, I'm all for Dad running a show because Mom will be happy that Dad will make more money to buy more eBay stuff and bigger yards and all, but that pitch meeting ruined a perfectly good night.

Fat Actress

I'm being stalked by a very ugly bitch. Boy, just because I lucked into a little money here, you wouldn't *believe* the skanks that come around. This one here has a body that would scare a cat off of a decomposing codfish. I told her I'd help her out, but *Jesus*! She's missing a couple of teeth and her breath stinks like the anal glands of a rhino.

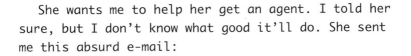

She wants me to help her get an agent. I told her sure, but I don't know what good it'll do. She sent me this absurd e-mail:

Dear Jinky,

I don't know if you remember me, but we met at Sunset Plaza a couple of years ago and you said if I ever came into town, I should contact you. Well I'm just out of rehab and I'm coming out to LA for pilot season! I hope you're as excited as I am about seeing each other. I've been living in New York, got close to getting a role, and went to producers and well, things are really moving for me now. I was wondering if you could help me get an agent out there. I'll be staying in West Hollywood and I can't wait to see you out there in sunny Caleefornia!

Love, Shirley ;)

Oh, boy. If Finley gets a load of her, she'll kick her ass. I just hope this scary monster isn't on meth and violent.

Pleasuring a Bug

Mom and Dad are having some problems. They came home from a premiere laughing about how bad the movie was and how strange it was seeing Arianna Huffington on a date with Gary Hart. While Finley and I chased the Stupid Kitty, Mom and Dad got into a fight.

Dad thought Mom looked really hot and wanted to do the crazy naked wrestling with her and she didn't want to. But Dad just went for it and Mom reacted the same way Finley would have reacted. Finley would have kicked my ass, actually.

Mom pushed him off, demanded some "romance" (whatever that means), and then Dad had another one of his tantrums. He ripped his pants off and *everything* in his pants pockets went flying around the living room. Then he stormed downstairs to his office, slamming all the doors on the way out, and lay on the couch in the dark, sulking for hours. This ruined our bedtime because we couldn't sleep without Dad in the giant bed. We waited and waited for him to come out of his "office" (the little guest house at the other end of the pool where he doesn't work).

The next morning, Mom demanded an apology.

Mom: "I think you owe me an apology."

Dad: "I'm sorry. But the micromanagement while we're wrestling is really annoying."

Mom: "That's really nice."

Dad: "I can't get the tongue movements delicate enough for you. It's like taking harmonica lessons from a Nazi."

Mom: "It's not that bad. C'mon."

Dad: "Yes it is. It's like trying to pleasure a bug."

Photo by Mark Kayne

My mom, the bug

Then Dad pretended to be a fly. He put on giant sun-glasses and flapped his wrists and made buzzing sound.

Dad: "The little tiny, teeny tongue movements are just too difficult. BZzzzzzzzzzzzzzzzz . . . oops, buzzzzzzzzzzzzzzzzzzzzzzzzzzzzzzzz. Sorry MBZzzzzzzzzzzzzzzzzzzzzzzz, sorry, excuse me."

Stress Pimples

Dad had to go and buy new tires for my '61
Studebaker. He almost didn't leave because of a
pimple on his nose. He just stood there again, staring at himself in the mirror in the living room as if
the people who sell tires are looking at Dad's skin
to see if it's good enough to buy a tire.

My Studebaker

Dad: "Why do I have a giant cherry at the end of my nose? It must be the coffee or the stress."

Mom: "Will you *stop*? Why don't you just stop touching your nose *all* the time? You should take Stri-Dex pads to work with you and stop shaking hands and touching surfaces and then touching your nose. Keep cleaning your glasses and your face with the medicated pads."

Dad: "Medicated pads? I'm not taking medicated pads to work! I'm working in a roomful of comedy writers. Do you know what kind of abuse I'll get if I take out medicated pads? I'll be like a honey-dipped rat in a cat factory."

Dad was so happy about his new joke that he forgot about his nose for five minutes.

Poor Mom and Dad. I wish they could see what it's like for just *one hour* on death row, where I came from. Then they'd know what stress is.

Boiling Mad

Photo by Nora Murphy

Dad's always complaining about something. Sometimes Mom feels like she ruined Dad's life.

Mom: "I know you'd rather be living by yourself up in Big Sur. You'd have no responsibilities, you could sell the house, get out of Hollywood, and go up there in some sordid cabin and date some divorced hippie who makes candles. You'd have plenty of money and you could lie around with a book on your chest and nap with your mouth open. . . . I'm just your ball and chain."

Dad: "You're not my ball and chain; *I'm* the ball and chain. You're the wind beneath my ball and chain."

Then Dad went to take a Jacuzzi in the dark. He's probably in there complaining while he boils in the hot bubbles.

I'm Cleaner Than Dad

I am not responsible for the ring around the tub. Dad is.

The best part of the tub experience is the weightlessness. Sometimes I make bubbles with my ass. Sometimes Dad does. I think that is one of his greater skills. He should stop reading those ridiculous books about writing and concentrate on the physics of water displacement with gas—a far more rewarding experiment.

17 October 2004

Our Hot Watering Hole Is Cool

Boy, do I like the Jacuzzi. I could spend several hours a day in there soaking in the hot bubbles. I'd like Finley to come in, but she just sits on the edge, taking in the steam.

She really should come in, though, because she's filthy. But she would turn the water into a kind of brown soup. Mom and Dad call it gravy. Finley's got greasy, wiry hair. When she walks, all the dirt and dust stick to her. I think she likes being dirty, which kind of turns me on.

Me and Dad in our very favorite spot

But I enjoy being boiled clean in a communal-type setup. As soon as Mom or Dad get in there, I have to join in. I like the whole Jacuzzi experience. It's the best of Hollywood. Dad says everything else about Hollywood makes you dirty.

Dad: "That's why my nose is breaking out. I've had it buried in Hollywood's ass for too long."

Big Hack Attack

We had another Hollywood pitch meeting at the house tonight. *Last Comic Standing*'s Gary Gulman was here with his manager and a bunch of other people.

They took over the couch right when I was trying to nap, then they all started stuffing their faces with giant globs of cheese and going on and on about how funny they think their show is.

I thought I might like the show when they said there was a dog in it. But the dog in the show is twenty years old and incontinent. Why would I watch that? They wouldn't watch a *human* that was a hundred and forty years old and pooping uncontrollably. I give that show one lifted leg.

Another thing that bothers me about the dog character on the show is how they talk about him. It's just wrong to make fun of him. What's funny about a dog slowly decomposing in the corner of a set on a sitcom? How many laughs can the lead character get tripping over his dying dog? How many canned laughs will they put in?

Not only that, these show biz dimwits never pay any attention to me when they come over here to *my* house.

That's it. Tonight, I'm making some demands. They are to serve me some melted cheese and make room for me on *my* couch. Another thing: They are to leave by 10:00 p.m., Minky Time!

Rain-Fresh Poodle Farts

It has been raining for three days straight and my yard is gooey and muddy. The ground is all spongy and mud seeps in between my footpads. It's kind of like a foot spa. The house is nice and muddy and we leave fantastic mud foot tracks all over the floors, carpets, and couches. The pool is overflowing and the paper lanterns outside look like used toilet paper wads hanging in the air. The people seem to like the rain (they say it's "romantic," whatever *that* means) but they're wearing rubber shoes and carrying *umbrellas*. What a useless encumbering

thing *that* is—a giant contraption they lug around to keep a few drops of water off their heads, where it feels good.

People. They'll spend thousands of dollars on a fake rain-shower head for their fancy bathrooms so they can have the *feeling* of rain but they don't wear umbrellas in there. And then if they're outside, and a little tiny raindrop falls on their head, they freak out. But under that phony shower in the bathroom, they're singing.

Everything is so fresh and clean when it rains, I can smell things going on miles away. Last night I smelled a BBQ in West Hollywood. I smelled a poodle fart from Burbank just now.

Bad Pitch

This morning Dad took us down the steep brick steps into the back part of the garden. It was foggy. Finn was rat hunting when Dad tripped on some soaking-wet moss. He got really mad like he always does and he threw his coffee cup against a tree and smashed it. Mom got mad because it was one of her antique cups.

Mom: "That's one of my Thai celadon antique cups! It's irreplaceable!"

Dad was in a bad mood because he and *Last Comic Standing*'s Gary Gulman pitched their big show to NBC yesterday and it didn't go well. He came home steaming mad last night.

Dad: "I'm through with these people. I've had it with this business. That's the worst pitch I've ever been to. It was like pitching in a sculpture garden. They just sat there. They didn't move a muscle. They knew before we even went in there that they weren't going to do this show. Why put us through that awful pitch? It's perverse! I can't wait to get the hell outta here and move to France."

I don't understand why Dad gets so mad. He's got it all. Why does he even care?

Dad: "I knew there was something wrong with this
whole setup when Gary wanted to work with *me*."

Then he moped around and called his agent to complain, but his agent had to take another call. That
agent guy gets paid 10 percent of Dad's money to
listen to Dad complain about show business once in a
while. I hope Mom gets paid a lot, because she has to
listen to Dad complain all the time about everything,
including his agent.

I think my ears might be designed for hearing complaints.

Every Pound Dog Is a Red Sox Fan

Last night *the Red Sox won* and that made everything good again. The Sox went to Yankee Stadium and did something that had never been done in baseball history. They came back from 0–3, tied the series, and forced a game seven. I'm happy because—let's face it—the Boston Red Sox are *the* underdog.

Every pound dog has to be a Red Sox fan. When I was on death row in San Pedro, I was at the bottom of the ninth, two outs, two strikes, and then I was saved.

The Red Sox are leading eight to one in game seven and I just got a whiff of somebody cooking something delicious in the neighborhood. Life is sweet.

Blue State Baloney

Mom and Dad are finally accepting the fact that Bush is going to be running the country for the next four years. They were pretty obsessive about it and threw an election night party that turned sour after Minky Time (my bedtime, 10:00 p.m.).

The house was full of depressed Hollywood types moping around and shoving food in their mouths while they watched the Red states bleed all over the map on CNN.

Dad: "Well, that's it. We've got a *moron* running the country into the ground for the next four years. A *monkey*! They elected him, they deserve him. We've got a bunch of liars and cronies in the White House!"

The more states they lost, the more they ate. They were loud and they took over the entire couch.

It really was a typical night here in LA—a bunch of liberals . . . drunk losers sitting in a mansion, *whining* about not getting their way.

I think the president dude isn't so bad. Look how he's always carrying that Barney around like an Italian man-bag.

Mom: "I know what you're thinking, Jinky, but *Hitler* liked dogs and you can't judge by that. The only reason that incompetent ass is carrying Barney off Air Force One is because Barney obviously doesn't *listen* to him. He won't come when he's called. *He* won't obey the president. Barney's the smart one."

Then Dad started yelling at the air as if the air could do something for him.

I still think I wouldn't mind hanging around with the president dude because he likes to hang around outside and vacation a lot on a ranch. I think that's *smart*. I know from experience that you can think better outdoors. I like the Bush dude—he likes dogs.

Actress Meat Puppets

Mom, the silly meat puppet

Mom took me to an audition this week. I sat in my bag on the floor. About thirty actresses were sitting there, talking to themselves. I thought they were crazy—turns out they were just rehearsing their parts.

Anyway, they were all way too old to be in microminis, but Mom said the role was for a sexy mom on *The Mountain*. These TV actresses had knees that looked like elephant knuckles.

All the ladies made cooing sounds when they noticed me in the bag. "Oh! Look! He's *so cute*," they said. "Look at his teeth!"

While they were admiring my underbite, I could see up every one of their skirts. There was a whole row of jumpy, twitchy legs, right in front of my nose, hoping to walk into that "producer session" and land a lousy role on TV.

I Will Bite Mon Dentiste

I've been told that I'm going to have to get my teeth cleaned. I guess my teeth aren't quite white enough—not up to Hollywood standards. I suppose braces will be coming soon. Mom and Dad have been discussing whether I should have my teeth cleaned here or in France. This is the crazy conversation that was the background for my nap last night.

Mom: "Jinky's teeth are filthy."

Dad: "I know. So are Finn's. Look at them. They're brown."

Mom: "We can't let it get out of hand, you know; if their teeth get infected, it could spread."

Dad: "I don't know how they're going to do Jinky. He'll bite the dentist. He can't wear a muzzle and get his teeth done."

Mom: "Maybe we should have it done in France."

Dad: "I've never noticed the dogs' teeth in France. Are they better?"

Mom: "I don't know."

Dad: "The people's teeth aren't so great."

Mom: "In France, they take better care of their dogs than themselves. Besides, it's cheaper there and they're used to dogs that bite. All medical stuff is cheaper in France."

Dad: "OK, we'll do their teeth in Nice."

Great. I'm really looking forward to the trip now. Can't wait to go to Nice for Christmas and have some Veterinazi halfway down my throat with scraping tools.

My parents are such hypocrites. Dad has canceled his last *seven* appointments with his dentist. He's supposed to go this Saturday but he'll probably flake. Mom skipped her last cleaning too.

My teeth are whiter than theirs anyway. And I'm not the one missing teeth. Dad is missing a tooth in the back and has a mouth full of crowns. Mom's had a bunch of root canals. I'd like to see either one of them rip apart a squeaky toy in one minute flat, like I can.

Finn Has a Tick on Her Lip

Finn has a tick on her upper lip and she won't let
anybody take it off. She must think she looks glamor-
ous with it because it looks like a mole on her lip.

Dad keeps approaching Finley with the tweezers,
but she runs away. When he catches her and holds her
down, she jerks her head around. Mom screams that Dad
is going to poke her eye out with the tweezers and
Dad gets mad because he hates to be told how to do
anything. None of us respond well to intructions or
commands in this house. Mom wants to try and get the
tick off Finley's lip with her nails but Finley won't
let her and Mom is afraid of being bitten, so the
tick/mole stays for now.

The tick *does* look kind of cool there on her lip except that it might have some kind of disease and it *is* sucking the blood out of her lip.

Last night, Finley was eating some chocolate Häagen-Dazs ice cream out of a bowl and Mom asked her, "Are you giving your tick some ice cream, Finley Finn Finn? That's nice of you."

Mom hopes that the tick doesn't get really fat in the middle of the night and decide to leave the host lip of Finn to crawl around on the bed in search of new lips. Mom would look cool with a live mole on her lip too. But Dad would think it looked better if it were on her boobs. I know him.

Dad Is Seven and a Half in Dog Years

Dad had a birthday and he is seven and a half in dog years. In people years, that's nearly dead. In Hollywood, that's a rotting corpse.

He's very pissed off because he only got three birthday cards and one of them was from BMW. The car salesman from BMW in Burbank sent Dad a birthday card even though he doesn't really know Dad.

Mom organized a birthday dinner at La Bohème, a restaurant in West Hollywood, and we didn't get to go because of the ridiculous hygiene laws in this country. Why can't we go and eat with our family on Dad's birthday?

This is how we celebrated Dad's birthday. Dad got on the big fun ball, Finn got on Dad, and I humped him like a madman.

The laws are all wrong. Our friends Graham and John can't get married because they're gay and we can't go to our own dad's birthday party, but *murderers* are allowed to get married and violent crazy people are allowed to buy automatic weapons. We're allegedly too filthy to walk into a restaurant but people are allowed to dirty up the entire air and whole rivers.

How are we any dirtier than the people eating in the restaurant? Is it our feet? Our feet aren't bringing in any different dirt than people's feet. And we don't spread tuberculosis (which is airborne) by coughing all over the place, like a lot of people do. We dogs don't spread colds, hepatitis, AIDS, smallpox, measles, or syphilis . . . like a *lot* of people in restaurants.

They need to take another look at these laws preventing us from enjoying Dad's birthday in a restaurant. We are welcome in every restaurant in Europe.

I fart on these law makers. I blow out my most virulent farty wind right in their face, in the direction of Washington, D.C.

Dad brought home a little white box called an iPod and Mom is now obsessed with downloading every loud and noisy thing they own so that they can bring the loud and noisy screeching to France in the little white box. These people waste a lot of time putting silly, useless stuff onto smaller and smaller techno-gadgets instead of running in the canyons or sitting in the sun. I love them, but their priorities are off.

Finn's Knitwit Getup

Mom has started a dumb new hobby—knitting. She's been sitting in the chair by the fire for five days straight, thrashing these knitting needles around like a madwoman. What a knitwit.

We were forced to go to the "Knitterie Parisienne" to buy yarn in "all the colors of fall" for Finley. Mom loves the place but the "Knitterie Parisienne" is actually on Ventura Boulevard, far from Paris and full of actresses. Mom has practically moved in there, she likes it so much.

These actresses sit around a table and knit tight sweaters all day under the watchful eye of a French knitting guru. This guru is treated like some sort of all-knowing high priestess of wool and philosophy. The scratchy yarn Mom bought is orange, brown, and rust. Fall is over, but Finn is going to look like a stuffed sausage who rolled around at the base of a tree in New England.

Mom is getting really frustrated with her new hobby because Stupid Kitty takes the ball of yarn while Mom is working on it and brings it downstairs. What Stupid Kitty does with it downstairs is a mystery but Mom runs down there screaming at the cat and comes back with an armful of orange mohair spaghetti, all in knots that she can't get out. I think she spends more time swearing at the knots in the yarn than she does actually making the stupid fall sausage sweater.

This weekend, we all had to go to an upholstery store instead of going to the park, to buy *pom-poms*!

Mom is apparently going to sew pom-poms around the sleeves of her new knitting project.

Dad was following Mom around the fabric store, while she cooed at every single different pom-pom color. Dad had that blank look on his face like he always does when she drags him out on shopping trips. He walks around in a circle, like he's in some sort of a daze, mentally avoiding the reality that we are in a fabric shop on Beverly Boulevard instead of a pub in Ireland. I know he's just happy that Mom is buying pom-poms, not apartments.

The sweater Mom is making for Finley isn't cheap. She's already spent over $100 just on the yarn. I like sweaters but I'm a plain, black turtleneck kind

I like the way it looks from the back—it's kind of like fetish-wear. Voilà la "derrière de terrière."

of guy, like Dad—not a pom-pom pansy. I hope she gets sick of knitting soon so that she doesn't make me a crazy sweater that makes me look like a clown. She's dressed us all up to suit her fantasies of fabulousness and we end up looking like a couple of queens, Dad and I.

Poodling in Nice

Finley, Mom, Dad, and I have been hanging around in the south of France, Europe, while Dad's show has been on hiatus. Mom's career seems to be on permanent hiatus.

Hiatus is great. It means I get to spend a lot of time with them doing nothing.

Dad calls it "poodling," which means hanging around idle and being useless like an old lady's poodle.

As soon as we got to Nice, France, Europe, Dad dropped his new Mac on the marble floor by the fireplace in the apartment. The laptop was smashed up and Dad had his first south-of-France fit—a Riviera temper

tantrum, where he smacked his head and yelled at the top of his lungs.

Dad: "Goddamnit! *How* much do I have to spend to get my goddamned e-mails? A million dollars? Is that enough? It's all because of *greed*! It's not enough to have a house in the Hollywood Hills. You have to risk getting on planes and having your *head* cut off by terrorists! You have to go and spend a *million* dollars so you can get an e-mail in *France*!"

Then Dad started running around the apartment holding the computer high above his head, threatening to hurl it out of the window.

Mom: "Shhhhh! The neighbors are going to hear you! Don't throw it out the window, maybe it can be fixed! Shhhhhh!"

Dad: "Let them get used to it! I don't give a god-damn who hears me. This computer can't be fixed. A brand-new computer! This is what happens when you get greedy and have to get online in *France*. We don't have a table, so I have to stand there at the marble fireplace and trip over wires. If we were at home, the thing would have been on a *table*! It can't be fixed. I'm going to kill myself. Arg! HHHHHARHG! Why? WHY?!"

While Dad stomped around the empty living room, which is like the size of the dog park off Mulholland in LA, Mom was able to fix the computer by gently bending it back and unbending the squashed plug so that it fit back into the computer port. It was like a miracle when she was able to turn it on.

The only thing that calmed Dad down was going out. We all got our coats on and walked to a store, where Dad bought some "poodle shoes." These shoes are made of exotic leather and are two-toned, with all kinds of crazy stitching on them. I don't know what the hell they are, but maybe they're made of special, extra-virgin unborn French snakes or something, they're so soft. Mom says they look like pimp shoes but he looked so happy walking around the store in his "poodles" that she didn't discourage him by quoting the euro/dollar rate that day.

Then we all walked over to the Parc Massena. For a change, Finley wasn't dragging like a ball and chain. Finley was out in front. It was warm for a February day, and Mom put her head on Dad's shoulder, and we strolled down the Rue de France to watch the sun go down over the Bay of Angels.

On the way home, I peed on three different historical monuments.

The Euro Pit

It was only our second night in Nice, France, Europe; we had just come back from a delicious mussel and *frittes* dinner and there was a note on the door from our neighbor, the old lady who lives right under us. There was an "important leak" in her bathroom, which is right under our bathroom.

Mom ran into the bathroom to check it out and she flushed the toilet, which is even older than the ancient lady downstairs. Then, brown goop bubbled up into the bathtub and two sinks. Dad was still in the entrance, trying to read the note in French.

Mom: "Oh my God! There's shit in the bathtub!"

Dad: "What the hell is going on? What is this about?"

Mom: "There's shit in the sinks and in the bathtub!
What are we going to do? It's a weekend!
Oh my God!"

Dad: "Goddamnit! Call a plumber."

Mom: "You can't call a plumber on a weekend in
France. They only work thirty-five hours! They
have weekends *off*, it's not like the States;
this is a *Socialist* country!"

Then Mom started to cry.

Dad: "Well, that's what you get when you want *two*
places to live. You get a bathtub full of shit.
That's the way it's going to be. I'm going to
work until I die and pay for a bathtub I don't
need in *France*! A bathtub full of shit."

Mom: "You hate it here, you hate France!"

Then the neighbors all came over to see what was
happening. They all smelled OK, no dangerous types,
just weird. I didn't feel like biting any of them,
even though they're French. They all told Mom and Dad
in French not to worry. They knew a plumber who would
come. Dad just stood there in the entrance surrounded
by our crazy neighbors who were all chattering in
French. He looked like he does when Mom is shopping—
shell-shocked and wobbling back and forth in one spot.

When the neighbors finally left, we went to bed, Dad muttering about how he was going to start calling the apartment the Euro pit.

Finley and I like the Euro pit, though. It's got really long hallways, so we can run and slide from one end of the place to the other. There are lots of good patrolling areas from the balconies. We can check out all activities outside and get a good look at all the neighborhood dogs.

French dogs are small and walk funny, like they've got something up their asses. Purebred snobby types, most of them. A lot of puny, nervous little candy-ass Yorkies. At home, very few dogs ever walk right within biting range. I think I'll kick some little French Yorkie's ass in the morning. I am an American, after all. Dad'll take me. He can't wait to get out of his Euro pit.

Fat French Finn

Mom and Dad are worried that Finn is ballooning in France with all the buttery croissants she eats every morning on the beach. Finn is so fat now that she is over the weight maximum for flying in the cabin. According to the stupid airline rules, we are only allowed to weigh ten pounds, but Finley weighs at least twenty.

Finn had her endocrine system checked out by some French quack vet on Rue Berlioz who told us that she has a surplus of growth hormone in her brain and that she will be a fat slob her whole life. Diagnosis: untreatable obesity. That's right, my wife is untreatably obese. I guess I'm no different than most guys. The vet had the nerve to tell me I have to keep her interested. The question ought to be how the hell is she going to keep *me* interested?

Dad has his own opinion about why she's fat.

Dad: "It's because we had her fixed. Ever since then she's gotten fatter. It's ridiculous. We weren't going to let her get *laid*."

I know we have a pet overpopulation problem but why can't bitches go on the pill? Mom thinks we can keep Finley's weight down by buying her new toys every day and keeping her excited (that must be how Mom stays in shape because she doesn't work out). The only thing that seems to get that lazy tub of lard to move is to buy crazy chittering squeaky toys. When she hears the toy screaming for its life, she runs over and does a lot of thrashing until the thing is dead.

Dad figures that because it takes her about a minute to kill a ten-euro toy, we're going to have to bleed thousands of euros just to be able to get Finley on a plane.

Getting fatter in France.
She looks like a walrus out there on the rocks.

Dead Dog Walking

Sometimes I don't know who I am anymore. I was Dead Dog Walking in San Pedro's shelter and here I am on the French Riviera. It makes you wonder. Just when you think you're gonna die, it's not your time yet.

A lot of people believe in all kinds of crazy stuff to make sense out of things but for me, it was the kindness of strangers. The world can be such a bad place and one tiny act of kindness can change everything.

Right now, I could wag my tail so hard it would knock the whole world over.

Oui, Oui!

There's a giant fire hydrant in the middle of Paris. It's fantastic! They call it the Eiffel Tower and every dog in Paris has peed on it. That's not all. The base of it is covered in dog poop. As soon as I got there, I marked it. *Oui, oui,* I made it mine.

They've got special French government poop guys who ride around on green motorcycles with a kind of dog-poop vacuum cleaner. They ride around the streets all day sucking up French poop, which is called *merde*, with their green hoses.

Mom always carries around baggies and picks up after me, which is more than I would do for her.

Karmic Mudslides

We're back in LA and it looks like it rained the whole time we were in France because there was a mudslide next door. The side of the hill fell down onto the house next to our pool and the people who live there had to move out. I think it might have to do with bad karma.

Dad doesn't believe they have bad karma but he's still mad at them for cutting down a whole row of our trees that were planted on the outside of our fence. The trees belonged to me and Dad and the neighbors thought the trees belonged to *them*.

Dad: (looking down the side of the mudslide at the house) "Trees would have helped."

Mom: "Don't be mean."

Dad: "But we had privacy from the road and now everyone can see us. *Criminals* can see our house. We had a beautiful row of trees, eighteen feet high, with flowers. They cut them down to the ground and now we've got a chain-link fence to look at."

Mom: "That's what happens when you cut down perfectly beautiful trees and plant a couple of ratty-looking cacti—what fools to plant cactus. How is *that* going to hold up a hill?"

On the way back from our walk, we ran into the neighbors and Mom and Dad made the same faces they make when someone is taking their picture. The neighbor told Mom and Dad how all the other neighbors had helped dig mud all night when the hill came down.

Dad: "We were in France. We just got back. Wow. That's terrible."

So we all had to stand there and look at the mud on top of their house for a long time while the neighbors complained about having to live with friends in another big house. Finley was so bored, she just lay down in the mud. I peed on the cactus plants, trying not to soak them too much.

If the neighbors had ever been nice to me at all, I would have helped them dig out mud. I *love* to dig in the mud.

Just as we got home, it started to rain again. I don't understand this karma thing but everybody in LA talks about it like it means something.

If it was true, then all of the bad people who are doing experiments on dogs like me—you know, the worst of the mean people who torture animals in laboratories—well, if karma really existed, then they would all die in mudslides but they don't. They're all fine and driving around in sports cars while the dogs they torture die in cages for nothing.

Cancer, Starbucks, and More Rain

There are mudslides going on all around us and it keeps on raining. Big rocks are all over the roads and the ceiling is leaking. Dad's TV show is off for a week and might get canceled because it's on at the same time as *American Idol*, so Dad has been hanging around the house all day in a dirty bathrobe. He gets dressed to go down the hill to Starbucks and to get the *New York Times* but then he gets right back into the stained bathrobe because the Jacuzzi is on.

Mom: "I don't know why you're going out, we have better, cheaper coffee here and the newspapers are all online. You're just running away from home."

Dad: "I'm the least successful writer on this street. They're all younger than me, they make more money than me, and they actually do something I have no idea how to do—they *write*."

Mom: "Well why don't you sit in your office and *write* something? You can write, you just don't want to."

Dad: "I'll never write anything as long as I live. I'm never going to do anything except do chores and clean cat hair off the kitchen counter over and over until I drop dead."

Mom: "Stop *talking* like that! You're not going to drop dead. *I'm* the one who's going to get

cancer. I'm going to get breast cancer and lose my tits and then you'll be sorry."

Dad: (putting on his jacket to go out) "I've already got diabetes. I'm going to lose a foot and then I'm going to get cancer and when I know I'm gonna die, I'm going to go and kill some people who have been bothering me. I've had it with people."

Mom: "Can you pick up some wet cat food and some salad stuff on your way back?"

I don't know what to do with these people. They need to go running in the canyons or something but it's hailing and there are sixty mile an hour winds out there. I try and cheer them up but that's the way they are.

Manhood and Criminals

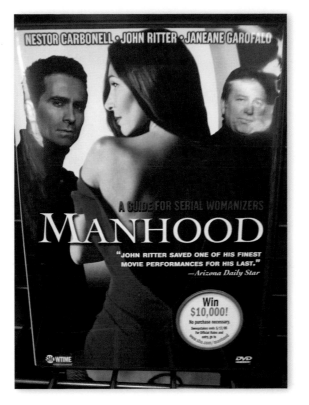

A picture of Mom in a red dress is on every video shelf in America this week. So today, Mom dragged us out in flash-flood conditions to go to the video store. We hung around at Blockbuster and watched a bunch of losers fingering the boxes with her picture on it. They'd read the box and then put it back on the shelf, like they didn't want to see the movie. I saw the movie when it came out and I fell asleep.

Mom and Dad were yelling all morning about it.

Dad: "They're obviously using you to sell the movie. At least they could give you credit. They give Tom Arnold credit, that lummox. They give Janeane Garofalo credit and they didn't use *her* picture on the cover."

Mom: "I can't get anything going in this town. Not even a cast credit on the box. The only thing I can get on the box is my ass. I've *had* it!"

I think Mom is overreacting. Nobody cares about her or this movie *Manhood* and none of it matters. I'll tell you what matters. The cops came up here after we got home and told us to be on the lookout for a "felon, twenty-nine years old, five foot nine, and wearing braces." He's somewhere around here and he might try to come into the house, so we're supposed to keep everything locked up. The cop told Mom to keep the phone handy to call 911 if we see the criminal.

I've got work to do. I'm patrolling the entire house and listening for any kind of noise. I'll kill him. Now that's *manhood*.

Going Out Wide

Last night we had *people* over again, blecch. I had *some* food from the table, but not enough. Whenever there are people here, we get less food, which makes no sense because there is so much more food on the table. It's like Mom and Dad are embarrassed to let me get up on the table in front of their Hollywood friends.

When it's just us at the table, I hang out and eat right out of their plates. I drink Mom's tea and I sleep on the table too. I drink wine and beer out of the glass. And I always do the prerinse cycle on the dishes before they go in the dishwasher. But when *people* are over, it gets all phony. We get stuck on the floor while Dad gives out all kinds of bogus advice about writing and Mom tells people exactly how to date.

Finley's smart. She doesn't want to hear it, so she goes to nap on the couch in the den, at the other end of the house.

What a bore they all were last night, gassing on and on about a script "going out wide" on Monday. "Going out wide" is when, instead of getting rejected one person at a time, you send your script to every-body and get rejected all at once.

Well, they went out wide, all right. They all ate so much they could hardly get out the door.

After everybody left, we all got into bed and Mom was hitting the bedsheets with the pillow.

Mom: "What are all these little rocks in here? It's like there's sand in the bed!"

I know what they are, those rocks. I've seen the cat go under the covers right after she gets out of the litter box.

Stupid kitty likes to plant litter in the bed when we're not looking.

February
2005

They Made Me Watch the Oscars

This was the worst Oscars show of my entire life. But every year, it's stupid. A bunch of idiots get all dressed up at noon and sit in traffic so they can go sit on their asses for ten thousand hours next to other idiots who are more famous than they are. Then, they all gas a lot about how great all the crummy movies are and give themselves statues and cry for the cameras. I think they do more crying and phony posing on that stage than they do in the actual movies. When they get on the stage, they take a really long time to thank a bunch of losers who didn't even get invited to the Oscars. Mom says that most of the people who were thanked will probably all be fired this week.

I've never seen any of them thank their dog, probably the only person in their lives who really cares about them.

You know what I can't figure out? There are a lot of animals in movies and they don't get awards, ever. They don't get credited. They don't get paid either. There are a lot of dogs and monkeys who have to act like clowns for these stupid movies. Horses have it the worst. All those old Westerns that Dad likes? Those horses are tripping and breaking their legs in every single movie. They're horror movies.

A friend of Mom's was here for the weekend with her little boy and they insisted on watching the Oscars with us. The kid sat on my couch in my spot, leaning his head on me like I am some kind of pillow

there for his enjoyment. He kept crying, "I'm hungry! But I'm hungry!"

During a commercial, Mom gave the kid a Popsicle to shut him up. He didn't even let me lick it once. I finally got some when a piece of it fell on the couch. It's a good thing I got it right away or Mom would have freaked out about the giant orange stain on the white couch.

I don't feel good about it but I kind of bit the little boy. I didn't bite down hard or anything but I just wanted to let him know I'm not that into him.

JAR Heads

A couple of times a year, Dad gets invited to dinner by his agent and Dad gets to choose the restaurant. This time, Dad wanted to go to Bastide, his favorite restaurant in LA, but his agent said it was too pricey. Actually, Bastide is just a really pretentious Hollywood trough where dinner is served in a hundred teeny courses and for what a dinner costs, you could pull a hundred dogs off of death row.

Mom: "The chef is an artist. He makes poetry with food. Fabulous, artful, creative, *extraordinary* food. That chef is a genius."

Dad: "Can you believe my agent wants to go to JAR because Bastide is too expensive?"

JAR stands for Just Another Restaurant, but Dad calls it Jerks and Rejects.

Mom: "You mean there's a restaurant in LA that's too good for you, after all the money you've earned for them? They didn't get you that writing job, *you* got that job and they just sit and collect! You ought to insist on going to Bastide."

Dad: "I bet Eric Roberts gets to go to Bastide. Who do you have to be to get to go to Bastide around here? I'm going to cancel dinner. He's ruined it for me. I can't go to Jerks and Rejects knowing that I'm not good enough to go to Bastide."

Mom: "No! Don't cancel dinner. That would make you look like a prima donna. Let's just go to JAR and you can tell him at dinner that you are a little shocked that there's a restaurant in LA that's too good for you."

Mom and Dad put us in our airline bags and we drove down Laurel Canyon to JAR. On the way down, we passed under all the red-tagged houses that are in danger of slipping off the mountain because of the rain.

When we go out to dinner in LA, because of the stupid hygiene laws, we're in the bag the whole time and no one knows we're there, so we get to see, hear, and eat everything. The bags are cozy with cushions and windows so when the food is served, Mom and Dad sneak us delicious, dripping bites of restaurant food.

As soon as we got to the table, Mom and Dad started behaving badly. When Dad's agent told Dad that he'd like to arrange a sit-down with a lawyer friend of his, Mom exploded.

Mom: "A lawyer? What a scam! These entertainment lawyers are thieves, ripping you off for 5 percent of what you make and they do *nothing*! They get paralegals to do all the work and you could pay someone by the *hour* to look over contracts!"

Then Dad started yelling.

Dad: "How many hours does it take to look over a contract? Five hours? Five *hundred* hours? What do they make an hour? A hundred thousand dollars? That's bullshit! Why should they make a percentage of what we make? They don't do anything! What about this? I give you 30 percent of what you make for me, not what *I* make! Go out and make me some money and I'll give you half of it, I don't care, but don't just take my money! $150,000 to look at a contract? I'll look at my own contracts. I know how to read contracts."

Then Mom asked the agent's girlfriend, who's also a writer, if she had a lawyer. She said yes.

Mom: "Fire him!"

Dad: "Yeah! Fire him! *He* does all the work! (Pointing at his agent) You don't need anyone else. Get rid of all these bloodsuckers."

People at the other tables were staring at us now. Finley was snoring but I was listening to the whole thing. I was licking some mashed potato off of Mom's finger when she started yelling at the waiter.

Mom: "Don't *ever* pour a new bottle into a full glass."

The waiter apologized and he said it was the same bottle.

Mom: "Yes, yes, it's the same *kind* of wine, from the same winery, but it's not the same bottle. Every bottle is different. You never pour two bottles in the same glass. Don't hate me, but you need to know this. It's not a refill on a Sprite, you know."

Dad: "Every bottle is a living thing. Didn't you see *Sideways*?"

The yelling got worse when the girlfriend said they were going to buy a dog.

Mom: "*Buy* a dog? Shame, shame, shame on you for buying when we kill millions of dogs a year in the shelters. You can adopt one, any kind you like!

I'll take you to the shelter myself and help you find one."

The agent's girlfriend: "Oh, I can't; it's too sad! I'll want to take them all home."

Mom: "What's sad is that they're going to die and you could take one. You don't have to take them all, only one. If you have room in your heart and your home for a dog, then it's awful if you buy one, knowing what goes on. You just *can't.*"

On this issue, I agree with Mom but there must have been a better way to convince her. Mom was acting like a rabid rottweiler.

At the end of the dinner, Mom went to the ladies' room. She strutted across the room and turned a lot of heads in her micromini skirt. When she came back, she told everybody at the table that the chef had stopped her in front of the bar.

Mom: "He grabbed me by both arms and pulled me toward him! And he said, 'What did you have? I might have made it.' I told him, 'I had a lousy bottle of wine and a dried-up piece of fish. Did you make that?' He let go of me like I was radioactive."

After dinner, Mom and Dad laughed all the way home. Big, loud laughing out of the open car windows. I think everyone in Laurel Canyon heard them laughing like a couple of hyenas. Even the coyotes, who make a hell of a lot of noise every night on their killing sprees, must have wondered what kind of monsters were coming up the hill in the middle of the night.

Jack Brussels Sprouts

Mom's moping around because she's "first choice" for another movie role. We met the director of *LA Confidential* last week and he really liked Mom but no call has come in yet. She is supposed to play Robert Duvall's girlfriend in a movie but Mom knows that "first choice" in Hollywood isn't worth one dried-up Purina pellet.

I don't want her going to Vegas and being away from the pack for months. I want her to stay here and cook.

Mom made a big dinner last night. She was all dressed up in high pointy shoes and every burner on the stove was red hot. All the pots were steaming with delicious people food. Dad was walking around in circles, moving the dust around the living room floor with the dust mop but Mom wanted him to do other stuff.

Mom: "Why are you dusting? There are a thousand other things to do before people come. *That* needs to be washed, *that* needs to be diced, *that* needs to be cleared up, and *that* needs to be dried so I can have room to do *this*."

Dad: "I guess every single thing I do is wrong."

Mom: "No, I just need help."

Dad: "I do a lot."

Mom: "Yeah, I know. You pay all the bills."

They always have stupid fights when they're nervous about not being ready for their food parties. This time, there was no time to fight because their guests started arriving.

It was better than most nights because this time, the Hollywood types that came liked me and Finn. One guy actually lay down on the floor to make out with Finley. She slipped him the tongue. There was a woman here who played with Zelda most of the night. I know she likes animals because she made a cartoon movie about sharks that showed sharks can be nice. Most movies about sharks show them eating people but this one showed a vegetarian shark fighting with his dad about eating fish. I saw her movie on the plane coming back from Nice. It wasn't bad. Thin story but great characters.

Everybody got drunk. It was past Minky Time (10:00 p.m.), I was trying to sleep, waiting to go to bed when they all started exchanging stories about losing control of bodily functions. I thought it would never end. It was horrifying.

Mom: (about Dad) "I can't believe how he walks around farting! If he makes any kind of effort, he farts. He can't even control his own ass!"

Dad: (about Mom) "The other day, she's in the Jacuzzi. I look at this beautiful naked woman in there. A vision. And then the giant gas bubbles. She's a very gassy lady. Phrffffft, phvvrrrrrrrooooooot!"

Mom: (screaming) "Ach! Stop it! *Stop* it! You're disgusting!"

Dad: "Yeah, she's in there floating on the surface
  bubbling like a powerboat."

Mom: "Stop!"

Dad: "*You* started it!"

  Then the guests all started with their stories.

Guest number one: "My mother can't stop farting.
  She's deaf, so she doesn't hear it."

Guest number two: "My grandfather was so full of gas,
  he was still farting an hour after he died!"

  I couldn't stand it. It went on forever. It was
disgusting. Why can't these people leave before Minky
Time (10:00 p.m.)?
  When they finally left and we got into bed, I positioned myself like I usually do, on top of the comforter, in the trench between Mom and Dad, my head
facing down, my ass up by their faces. For making me
stay up so late to listen to their horrible stories,
I blasted them with some hot air of my own.
  Dad calls me Saddam Hussein when I do that,
because he says I gas my own people. Then he fans it
over to Mom's side of the bed.

Dad: (fanning with both hands) "There."

Mom: "Ucch! Why are you doing that?"

Dad: "So you can enjoy the delicious Jack Brussels
  Sprouts."

Dad likes my Jack Brussels Sprouts; I can tell because he always smiles when I send one his way.

You never know what the bubbles are in there.

Hurty Balls

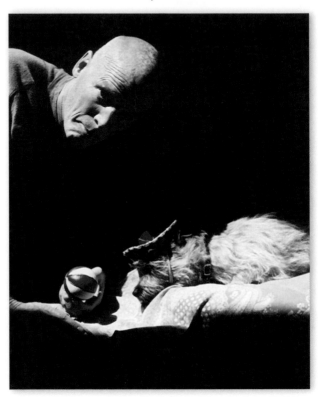

We have lots of balls in the house.

I think Dad carries some kind of very delicate balls in his pants. I no longer have balls because they had to be cut off, so I don't remember how hurty they can be if you just bang into them the wrong way.

I saw a huge Labrador walking past our car in the parking lot at Whole Foods on Fairfax and I jumped over to the window on the driver's side to yell at him. I stepped on one of Dad's balls by accident and he screamed almost as loud as when he dropped his new Mac on the marble floor in France.

I'm glad I don't have those kinds of hurty balls. I've got all sorts of other balls, though. Balls you can slam against walls without anyone screaming like that.

Dad's always accusing Mom of breaking his balls. I know Mom would like to get rid of Dad's balls altogether but he won't let her.

Exotic Hairless Guests

A hairless Chinese guy has moved into the neighborhood and I don't like it. Finn is very interested in him and she makes all kinds of flirty cooing sounds when he's around. Mom invited the Chinese hairless guy and his mom to lunch and as soon as he walked in, he lifted his leg and peed on the living room floor.

I don't think he's any kind of serious threat to me and I'm way more buffed than him. Plus, he's got really creepy skin that gets pimples and sunburn, just like people. But Finn thinks he looks like a rock star, so I might have to kick his ass.

The Chinese crested guy and his mom both talk a lot but neither one of them makes much sense. His mom tried to convince my mom that dead people can be reached through a channeler but my mom thinks that channelers are a bunch of quacks.

Chinese hairless's mom: "Don't you dream about people who have died?"

Mom: "All the time!"

Chinese hairless's mom: "Well, that's how the dead come to you! They come to you in your dreams!"

Mom: "Really? I thought that dreams were just random neurological synapses that play bits of memories in shuffle mode—sort of like an iPod with personal data you've downloaded over a lifetime. No dead person has ever tried to reach me. They're . . . dead. Even most *live* people I know don't try to reach me."

Then the hairless guy's mom made him play dead. He got on his back and put his legs up in the air but his head wouldn't completely touch the floor. So his mom held a piece of rigatoni up in the air and started barking out the order to play dead.

Chinese hairless's mom: "Dead dog, dead dog. Come on, dead dog! **Dead dog**!"

I thought it was pretty weird that this woman was forcing her dog to pretend he was dead, just so he could get a piece of rigatoni. Finley didn't like it at all. She thinks it's degrading when people force dogs to "play dead." I think the Chinese guy lost a little of his rock star appeal when he groveled for a noodle in front of Finn.

Dad plays dead a lot in the Jacuzzi. He puts his head underwater and stays there floating, not moving for a long time, which worries me. All I can see is his back and the top of his head. Now that I think about it, the skin on Dad's head is all freckled. It looks like the hairless Chinese guy's skin.

Mom always laughs when Dad plays dead but I don't think it's funny. If Dad died, I'd want to die with him. I'll tell you what, though, I wouldn't mind seeing that Chinese guy floating in the pool.

I don't know what Finn sees in this guy. Look at his skin. He looks like a cross between Michael Jackson and Andy Warhol. He needs moisturizer and his pee-pee looks like an eraser head.

Coyotes!

This week there are houseguests from France living in all of the bedrooms. Whenever we have houseguests, Mom gets nervous about us getting out and being eaten by coyotes. Mom has put big signs on all the doors in the house that say:

PLEASE KEEP DOOR CLOSED BECAUSE COYOTES ARE HUNGRY.
DO NOT LET ANIMALS OUTSIDE.

These signs are useless because people never read the signs and they leave doors open all over the place. Mom doesn't realize that we don't like to go out without our people anyway and Stupid Kitty doesn't dare to go past the driveway when she sneaks out. She's too much of a coward to go anywhere. Still, Mom has horrified the houseguests with details of cats she knows who were ripped limb from limb in the neighborhood and screaming Maltese dogs being murdered right in front of their helpless owners by gangs of blood-thirsty coyotes. Mom thinks up all kinds of scenarios, like a hawk swooping down and sinking its claws into Stupid Kitty and then pulling her up into a tree to devour her. I *like* that scenario.

Mom: "You'll hear the coyotes at least once a week in the middle of the night. You'll hear the pack howling like this: Aiyah! Ya! Ya! And then you'll hear the bloodcurdling screams of a little cat or dog dying. It's awful. We hear it all the time."

It's true, we *have* heard a few gruesome sounds out there in the dark but I wish Mom would learn how to relax and stop scaring the houseguests from France. We're not stupid enough (Finn and I) to go looking for trouble in the woods up here in the middle of the night. Mom should eat a giant bowl of yummy food and then take a nap in the sun and stop filling her mind with visions of our entrails spilling out all over the floor because we're all going to die one day anyway, and it'll be much later and it won't be so bloody and crazy. We'll all just get old and fall into a giant sleepytime that we won't wake up from.

Dad, protecting us from coyotes

Marco-Schiavo the Marcoleptic

I *really* like one of the houseguests. He's Mom's
godson, so in a way, he's related to me. His name
is Marco but Mom calls him Marco-Schiavo because he
sleeps most of the day (there's a woman named Schiavo
who's been in a coma for years and she's a big TV
star right now). Dad sayes Marco sleeps so much he's
inspired a new disease, Marcolepsy. When he's awake,
he's so much fun because he thinks like a dog. Nothing matters except what's happening right now. He
knows the important question in life: Is it fun?

I wish he would take me when he goes out so I could party with him. He must be the top dog in the Hollywood nightclub scene because he's tall and has really long eyelashes with huge eyes that are the color of grass after the rain. He wants to become a writer and live in Hollywood, which means I'll get to hang out with him.

Marco-Schiavo and Mom have been hanging around the pool together, writing a horror movie about a sweet-looking grandmother who is a pedophile sex offender. They laugh all the time. You know, when I look at Mom, who's kind of old, working with her godson who's kind of young, their idea about a granny sex offender is kind of close to the surface. Creepy.

Marco-Schiavo sneezes a lot, so, in case he's contagious, Mom makes him wear rubber gloves when he checks his e-mails on her computer. He's pretty cool about it. Whenever he has to get online, he just puts on the crazy yellow rubber gloves.

I think Marco-Schiavo might have more than a head cold. He could be sneezing a lot because Stupid Kitty sneaks into his room and rubs her ass all over his clothes when he's sleeping. I've watched her do it.

A Dude Named Pope

A dude named Pope died on TV. He's got an awful lot of friends in long red dresses. It's weird to see a bunch of *guys* wearing long red skirts with lace following the Pope guy's corpse around for days. He must stink pretty bad by now because one of the men in red keeps swinging an incense burner over him.

Mom doesn't like him very much.

Mom: "He's got *blood* on his hands! How can he go to Africa and Asia, where people are dying of AIDS, and tell them not to use condoms? And why can't women be ordained? We're a bunch of breeders to him, no more . . ."

I wonder what Pope thinks about the Spay/ Neuter thing. Does he ever think that we've got too many homeless animals dying in cages by the millions? Are there dogs in heaven? Did Pope Dude ever have a dog? And why aren't there any dogs at the funeral?

Pope had the biggest parties I've ever seen. And his car was so cool because he could ride around without birds pooping on his fancy dresses. His house is *very* fancy but the yard is terrible. All stone and no trees, no grass, no shade, not even a shrub.

I guess people are crying because they'll miss Pope riding around in a gold hat with his hands up in the air talking about stuff they wish they could do but don't. It's the biggest bunch of guilty-looking people I've ever seen. At least in Hollywood they don't feel bad about the stuff they do.

These guys in long red dresses can really sing. They sing this beautiful, sad song, where they call out the names of all the saints. (If I understand it right, saints are dead people who saw dead people and spoke to more dead people.) Dad's been making fun of them, walking slowly across the living room with a red towel wrapped around his waist and a white napkin on his bowed head. He sings the song in Latin, except he changes the names of the saints to Italian food.

Dad: "Oh, oh, oh, oooooooooh, Santo Spirito Spaghettini . . . Oh, oh, oh, oh, Santo Spirito Scungili . . ."

This drives Mom into a laughing frenzy, where she can't even catch her breath.

Dad: "Oh, oh, oh, Santo Spirito Rigatoni . . ."

Back in Nice, France, Europe

We're back in Nice, France, Europe. What a great place. There's a sea breeze that comes off the Bay of Angels and right into the living room. If I hold my head in the right position, I can sniff things all the way to North Africa. I can smell unbeliev-able food all around me and I get to go into all the restaurants, where they serve me dripping morsels of fabulous food.

I might just stay here and get fat like Finn.

We have the biggest dog bed I've ever seen and our food bowls are from Morocco. The sun shines every day

and we have balconies facing two different streets, where Finley and I can patrol all sides of the house for dogs that might approach our territory.

There are so many French dogs here that we work most of the day enforcing our airspace. When a dog walks by, we go into attack mode and run for the balconies.

The wrought-iron balconies look like they were made for us, because they have openings that are exactly the size of our heads. We stick our heads out and we bark as loud as we can at all the French poodles and Yorkies. We make sure the French dogs know that they are passing U.S. territory. We make sure that if they mark the street, we go and mark on top of what they marked.

Dad's Show Got Canceled

The day after we arrived in Nice, France, Europe, Dad's show got canceled and he's walking around like we'll never be able to get any more food.

Mom told me not to worry, that we have enough to buy food for a long, long time. I'm not worried about the food so much but I'm worried about Dad. He takes out his calculator a thousand times a day and makes lists of expenses. This drives Mom crazy because she can't count and Dad always wants her to count.

Mom: "Don't ask me to count!"

Dad: "You can spend money all day long but you can't listen to me for *two* minutes about what everything costs around here?"

Mom: "I'm no good at math!"

Dad: "It's not math. You don't have to be Einstein to know what you're spending. Math. We need to make a *list* of everything. The shutters, the paint, the plumber, the electrician, I'm bleeding money!"

Mom: "Oh God. Here we go again. Just remember. When the euro goes up, the dollar goes down. When the euro goes down, the dollar goes up. And if you can't take the stress, just sell this place."

Dad: "No, I love it here. This place is great. I'm going to learn French and I'm going to swim and I'm going to join the gym. And I'm going to get a bike. And work out."

Dad's been talking about working out for as long as I've known him. I think I saw him pick up a fifteen-pound weight a year ago. He lifted it a couple of times, said "Ow!" and put it right back in the rusty pile of free weights by the pool at our house in Hollywood.

Here in the south of France, the only thing Dad lifts is his calculator. He likes to take his calculator out for walks. He takes it and his list of expenses and he goes to the *LAVE CLUB*, which means "wash club" in French.

Dad: "I should live in a van. I'm bleeding money and all I do is chores. I spent a *million* dollars to do chores in French."

Mom: "France is all my fault. This apartment is my fault and the euro going down is also all my fault. You hate me."

Dad: "I don't hate you. I love you. But it's difficult."

Then Mom leans all over me while I'm trying to nap.

Mom: "Look how cute that Minky is. Look at him. He's adorable!"

Dad: "Oh, that Minky-mink. Minky-aw, Jinky-aw, Binky-aw!"

Really, all I have to do is sit up and blink at them and they make a big fuss over me and forget all about the dumb fight they just had. I have a strange power over them. If I open up my eyes so that the whites show at the bottom, they get weak in the knees and start cooing like a couple of idiots.

Mom's an Invalid and Dad's Unemployed

Waiting for Mom to come home from the hospital

The very next day after Dad's show got canceled, Mom broke her foot. We were coming out of the bank on Avenue Jean Médecin and she stepped on a curb wrong and tripped. I heard her foot snap in two. *Ouch*!

Mom yelped and Dad had to call an ambulance. It was the scariest thing seeing them carry Mom into the back of an ambulance because I didn't know where they were taking her and they wouldn't let me come!

Dad was really worried about her. He loves Mom almost as much as he loves me.

Dad stood on the balcony for hours watching for her to come home. Finley and I waited with our heads out of the balcony railing for the whole day until she finally came home, crying and on crutches.

Mom: "I *never* should have worn flat shoes! I've got a theory: When you're wearing high heels, you are careful about where you step. When you're wearing *sensible* shoes, you think nothing can happen, so you run around on cobblestone streets like they were an Olympic track! I've climbed the cliffs of the Amalfi Coast in my highest Manolo Blahniks and nothing happened. I'll never wear flats again!"

So now Mom stays home a lot because of her broken foot and everybody has to be careful not to knock Mom over on her crutches. I kind of like her broken foot because we get to hang out on the couch and be all cozy with her.

It's funny how sometimes the things that people think are bad things, like Dad's show getting canceled and Mom's foot getting broken, are really *good* things. Dad losing his job only gives him more time to do what he wants to do. He wants to spend time with me and he wants to nap and read.

Mom's broken foot is making her a better person. It's forcing her to be more patient . . . to appreciate things more. She's talking to people she never would have met before. She has all kinds of new friends at the dog park—old ladies on crutches and walkers. She's finally understanding what's important in life. The simple act of walking to the beach or to the park . . . with me.

Just between you and me, Mom and Dad needed a kick in the ass.

Depression Niçoise

Dad is feeling grumpy and Mom thinks he should *do* something to snap himself out of it. Last night, Dad went to bed before the rest of us and sat in the dark.

Mom: "What's wrong *now*?"

Dad: "Nothing. . . . I'm out of it, that's all. I'm tired. I'm bleeding money, I'm not working, and all I'm doing is buying more towels and sheets . . . in *France*."

Mom: "Well, why don't you *do* something? You've been talking about getting a French bike for months. Why don't you just buy the bike and go for ride? Take *my* bike. Work out, join the gym! You could bleach your teeth, you've been talking about bleaching your teeth for years."

Dad: "I'm too depressed to bleach my teeth."

Mom: "Why? You've brought the tooth-bleaching kit everywhere for two years now and you never do it. It's always in the suitcase for nothing. Bleach them now."

Dad: "It's too depressing. I have to wear glasses to see to put the droplets of bleach gel in the tooth tray. Might as well be sitting here in my truss with glasses on. Like Ben Franklin trying to get Brad Pitt's teeth. If I bleach my teeth it'll just be scary. It'll be like Wink Martindale's teeth superimposed into Gollum's mouth. I'm not bleaching my teeth."

Mom: "What's a truss?"

Dad: "Look it up."

Mom: "We don't have an English dictionary in France."

Dad: "It's a thing to hold up your herniated ball."

Poor Dad. I think I'd better pretend I need a walk. Then I'll drag him four blocks to the beach. He'll feel better in the salt air of Nice, France, Europe. We can pee in the sea together and mark the Mediterranean.

Hollywood Invasion in Nice, France, Europe

I thought that Hollywood was on the other side of the sea and way across the land from Grandma's house in New York, but for the last week, Hollywood has come here to Nice, France, Europe. More Hollywood people have invaded my house.

A TV hack and his phony, swishy husband have come to stay in my kitchen, on my bed, and on my giant dog bed in the living room. They're hanging around on my balconies and they're in the way of my important patrol work.

The restaurant in Èze, where we'll never be allowed back because of some Hollywood people and their dog

I can't stand it. I might have to bite them. Especially the one who pretends to be a princess.

The TV hack and his princess husband have closed off the back bedroom and bathroom, which is in my patrol area. That's where my favorite bathtub is, where I like to drink out of the leaky faucet. I can no longer get to that bathroom because I might put "my dirty feet on the tub."

They've brought an unruly whippet dog who thinks *my* house is a toilet. The unruly dog doesn't just think my house is his toilet, he thinks hotel lobbies and restaurants are *all* toilets. And his parents think it's great. I guess they're just happy that he isn't actually pooping on them.

Unruly dog's dad: "He likes to shit on *marble*! Isn't it wonderful? He likes to pee where it's luxurious! Isn't that just FABulous?"

No, it isn't. Then dogs won't be allowed anywhere anymore.

Unruly dog's dad: "He peed in the fountain! Isn't it wonderful?"

No, that's where I *drink*.

These Hollywood dummies have some silly ideas. They believe that dogs should never eat people food. Where do they get these ideas? People are supposed to be smart. Dogs have been living with people for millions of years. Do you think they had Science Diet Lite sawdust pellets for sale at PetCo outside a stone cave in Africa in the year 1 million BCD (before Christ's dog)? People and dogs have been sharing meals before they ever made a single Hollywood movie.

It just doesn't make any sense that you would let someone *poop* in a museum but not let him eat a croissant.

The other night, we went to one of our favorite places high up in the cliffs of Èze. This is a place where they always bring me and Finn stuff to eat and a big pail of mineral water. While our parents droned on and on over disgusting black fish eggs and champagne, the unruly dog peed on the terrace. Neither of his two dads would clean it up and I was scared the restaurant people might think it was me.

Mom: "Did you clean it up?"

Unruly dog's dad: "Well, it was outside, wasn't it?
     They'll never know. It'll evaporate."

I wish they could figure out that we *live* here and if the waiter thinks *I'm* the one who peed there and made him clean up a giant puddle of pee, I'll never be allowed to come back.

Then the people gassed on about American television while their dog chewed up the table leg and Finn and I tried to nap.

Unruly dog's dad: "Don't you just love that show *Desperate Housewives*?"

Mom: "No."

Unruly dog's dad: "Why? We *love* it!"

Mom: "I can't look at that show without thinking I
    should be on it but I can't even get an audi-
    tion for that show, so I can't watch it without
    feeling sick."

I don't know how long these show biz people are going to stay but I hope it isn't like in Los Angeles,
where people only leave when they get a better offer.

Drinky Jinky

I've been drinking.

Maybe it's the French influence—I don't know, but the water in the bowl on the floor just doesn't interest me anymore.

I think the drinkies started when we got to Nice, France, Europe. I was on the dinner table one night and drank some beer out of Mom's glass. I walked over to the other end of the table and dunked my snout into

Dad's glass, which had a nice heady Barolo red wine. I like that stuff too. The local wines aren't bad at all and they cost little more than two bags of cat litter.

So now, every night during dinner, I go back and forth from one end of the marble table to the other, eating out of their plates and drinking out of their glasses. Mom and Dad think it's "adorable."

Now it's gotten to the point where I demand an aperitif. Mom's got some delicious new stuff called Pineau des Charentes. It's sweet and sticky and I love it more than any other drinky.

By the time dinner starts, I've got a good buzz going. Being drunky from the drinkies makes me happy.

Mom: "Look! He's drinking! It's so adorable! Do you *like* the drinky, Jinky?"

Dad: (laughing) "We can't let him become an alcoholic, though."

Mom: "Oh, please. Growing up in France, they always put wine in my baby bottle with the water! I didn't become an alcoholic."

Dad: "He's just like his daddy. He *likes* it."

Mom is half French and she's been drinking wine since she was born. But Mom and Dad never let me drink as much as I'd like to. And Mom doesn't let Dad drink as much as *he'd* like to either.

Everybody is always trying to control everybody around here and it never works.

Finley has simpler tastes. She just likes meat and mice.

Life's a Bowl of *Moules*

Look at me. I've got the greatest pillows in Nice, France, Europe.

But enough about Mom's pillows, I'm bored with them—and so is everybody else by now, I think. What I'm really into lately is *moules*.

Moules, or mussels, in wine and butter sauce. *Moules* in tomato sauce. *Moules* with caramelized onions. *Moules* sautéed, baked, or in soup—I'm crazy about *moules*! I will sit here and Mom will drop them into my mouth until I get sick.

Mom says they cost about the same as dog food in the States. I think that's why Dad loves them so much, because they're really cheap and you can order a bucket of them for the price of a bag of cat litter.

The great thing about *moules* is that they have to be eaten right away. You can't take them home and eat them the next day.

Mom: "How can something so good turn so bad the next day?"

Dad: "I guess you haven't dated much."

House Hunters in My House

Here's a "candid" picture of Mom getting ready for a dumb-ass real estate TV show. The hat and sunglasses indoors look pretty stupid. She forced me to smile for some Roblochon cheese. I'll do just about anything for some Roblochon cheese.

Mom's career must be making its final death rattle because she's agreed to do an episode of HGTV's *House Hunters*. The show is coming to Nice, France, Europe to film a bunch of expats here in their new hundred-year-old houses.

The idea of a film crew coming in here and rear-ranging all my furniture to make it look like we

don't live here yet is so fake. Then they'll put it all back and Mom and Dad will talk about how fabulous everything is here in Nice, France, Europe. What the producers at *House Hunters* should film is all the endless complaining Mom and Dad do. Then it might actually be a *real* reality show.

Mom: "I can't believe I've come to this . . . doing a cheesy HGTV show. How much worse is this going to get?"

We found out pretty quickly. Mom's agent called from Hollywood last night. I heard the whole thing.

Mom: "So I haven't missed anything earth-shattering, right? Nothing's happening?"

Mom's agent: "No, it's been pretty dead here this summer. There hasn't been anything life-changing, it's real quiet but things should be picking up for your type as soon as you get back. Lots of good stuff coming up . . . lots of good stuff."

I know what "lots of good stuff" means in Hollywood. It means that Mom is going to have to spend hours memorizing pages of ridiculous lines and then leave the house all day to meet with idiot producers who then tell her agent that they loved her but wanted someone more famous than her for their crappy TV show.

To top it off, the *House Hunters* people never showed up. The show Mom thought she was too good for? They never even showed up.

Human Waste

Mom and Dad are never going to have human babies. A study came out that said that Dad's sperm might cause Down syndrome and schizophrenia because he's old. Mom has always wanted to have a human baby but she can't. I think Finley and I are the only babies Mom will ever have. Every month, when she's ovulating, she gets overly mommy-ish, like she's missing something.

Mom: "I'm telling you, it's my last egg coming down. You'd better try and fertilize it."

Mom's furry baby, Finn

But Dad was busy writing his list of things to do before he dies.

Dad: "I'll never get to do any of these things. I'll be lucky if I organize my underwear drawer. And then I'll be dead."

This morning, Mom was in the bathroom a long time, reading a giant book on the Algerian war. Dad came in.

Dad: "Hi, Jinky!"

Mom: "Can you please give me some privacy, get out, and close the door?"

Dad: "What are you doing, having an ass baby?"

Mom: "The only baby I'll ever have."

Dad: "Too old to have any other kind of baby."

Mom: "That's not true!"

Dad: "Maybe if I can squeeze out the last few drops of damaged baby sauce, you can have a real baby. One that will have to live in a cage . . . but human, kind of."

Mom: "You're revolting. Get out. Let me finish my book."

Dad: "It's taking you longer to read about the war in Algeria than it took them to fight it."

Romanian Attack Orphans

Mom and Dad have some friends who live in Monaco and the wife, Valerie, is a big movie producer in France. Valerie and Pierre (a French cinematographer) have adopted an eight-year-old girl from an orphanage in Romania and Mom would like to adopt a human baby too because she can't make one herself. Her oven's broken. Dad doesn't want any human babies, he's happy with dogs.

Valerie and Pierre were here for dinner last night but in the middle of dinner, Valerie's cell phone rang. Right away, everybody at the table knew there was a major problem. They all got very quiet to hear the call, which was from the English nanny. I heard the whole thing, even the tiny voice of the nanny, because I'm a dog and can hear hundreds of times better than humans.

Nanny: "The nasty little minger bit me! She bloody bit me on the tit!"

Valerie: "Oh, no! I'm *so* sorry. Put her on the phone right away. (Then to Pierre) She bit the nanny."

Nanny: "Get over here *now*, you cow, and talk to your mother. You're in big trouble."

Then the Romanian orphan got on the phone and yelled so loud, everyone at the table heard it.

Romanian orphan: "You'd better fire this whore *now* or

I'm going to cut myself! I'm going to swallow all the pills in the medicine cabinet unless you come home right *now*!"

Valerie: "Calm down, darling, Mummy will be home in a few minutes. Try to relax. Play with your Disco Barbie. Put that new outfit on her and Mummy will be right back."

Pierre and Valerie got up from the table.

Mom: "She bites? Oh my God."

Valerie: "It's awful. She has an attachment disor- der and she bites my breasts. She almost bit my nipple off! She hits me as hard as she can and she hasn't looked me in the eye for years. I'm covered in bruises."

Dad: "Can't you give the kid back? Return it?"

Valerie: "We can't give her back. It's ruined our *lives*. We haven't had a relaxing weekend in years. She's been biting us ever since we got her out of Romania."

Mom: "Oh my God! What are you going to do?"

Pierre: "She bit the last nanny and she quit. At least here, the nannies don't sue like in the States. It's been a tremendous strain."

I couldn't believe what I was hearing. A dog would be put down for this stuff.

Pierre: "I'm sorry, guys, we're going to have to go. We've got a situation. Come on, Val."

After they left, Mom and Dad were cleaning up in the kitchen and having espressos. Finley and I were helping out by doing the prerinse cycle on the dishes, licking up all the leftover sauce, and getting them ready for the dishwasher.

Mom: "What if we adopted a little girl from Bangladesh, a four- or five-year-old? We could give her a life."

Dad: "Didn't you hear Valerie? They *bite*!"

Mom: "They don't *all* bite!"

Dad: "*Ours* would. It'll grow up and burn the house down and murder us. Forget it. No way."

Mom: "Jinky bites. You want to return him?"

Dad: "He bites *other* people, to protect us. If I could get a kid who would only bite burglars— like an attack orphan—then maybe."

Mom: "But *ours* wouldn't turn out like that, we'd have an adorable, beautiful little girl who could have a wonderful life with us! There are so many who need loving homes. They're just waiting for someone to love them, like dogs at the pound!"

Dad: "No! I'm not getting anything you can't take *back*. With our luck, the kid would steal all

my money and become a criminal. I'm not adopt-
ing some ex-commie pyromaniac crook. Let's just
stick to dogs."

Mom: "Oh, come on. You're being harsh."

Dad: "No really, did you ever think that we're not
supposed to have kids? That maybe our bodies are
refusing to have kids to save us? Our bodies are
trying to save us from making a terrible mistake!"

It's just as well they're put off by the biting Romanian orphan. They couldn't handle a child.
They're too immature.

I Love NY

On our way back to Hollywood, we stopped in Mom's hometown, Manhattan, to see my grandma.

Grandma's apartment is right near Central Park, where we're allowed to run off the leash until 9:00 a.m. So in New York, we have to get up *really* early to go squirrel hunting. I would like to start at 1:00 a.m., but Mom and Dad won't go for it.

Manhattan squirrels are too smart to get caught. They know the time. They know that dogs have to be back on leash at 9:00 a.m. or their people get a ticket for $250. So the squirrels don't come down from the trees until it's ticket time.

They look us right in the eye from up in the trees and laugh at us, those New York squirrels. They're kind of like the people there—too smart, living way up high, looking down at the rest of us and laughing.

N.Y. squirrel: "Hey, you! Hey! You tink you can get a piece of me, huh? Fuggetaboudit. You tawkin' to me? I dare you to come ovah here an' try it. I'll give you duh rabies if you even *tink* aboudit. Come ova here—I'll shit on you, you mangy, cookie-begging, jerky-eating bastard."

They're kind of *fun* crude in New York.

Every time we go to Grandma's in New York, there's either a heat wave or a snowstorm. Being at Grandma's is like living inside an oven. She doesn't have an air conditioner because she thinks they're ugly.

Grandma: (Grandma's French) "Zay are *ugly*! I'm not going to ruin my windows! Eeeets only two weeks a year zat eet is zees hot."

Mom: "How can you stand it?"

Grandma: "Use zee Vornado!"

Grandma has a superpowerful fan called a Vornado. It doesn't oscillate and you have to be sitting right in front of it to get the full G-force effect of it. Of course, Finley hogs the Vornado and the rest of us just sit there in the heat and complain. Every couple of hours, the Vornado gets so wound up, it explodes, and BANG! Pieces of the fan fly around the room like a bomb. Then Dad has to spend a half hour sweating, putting it back together again.

Even in the winter, Grandma's place is like an oven because they have some crazy kind of heating system that whistles like a train and fills the whole apartment with steam.

I love visiting Grandma in New York. The food there is amazing. It's a very interesting place. The dogs all have nannies and flashy jeweled collars. They're well dressed, well groomed, and cultured. They're almost all expensive purebred dogs who pick the right stocks and eat take-out from Zabar's.

It's very different from Hollywood, where people are always fake smiling and telling other people to have a nice day. In New York, they look elegant but they say what they mean.

Dad got into the New York state of mind with a nasty butterball in exercise pants on West 86th Street. Finley was pooping in the gutter, Dad had her on the leash, and he didn't have the baggies to pick it up. Mom had the baggies and she was talking to an old friend of hers in front of Grandma's.

Butterball in stretch pants: (sneering at Dad) "Pick it *up*!"

Dad: "I'm going to. (To Mom, halfway down the block) Hey, Honey! Do you have the baggies?"

Butterball in stretch pants: "I *said*, pick it *up*!"

Dad: "It's in the *gutter,* for God's sake. It's a walnut-sized poop and my wife has the baggies over there, down the block. Do you think I should pick it up with my bare hands?"

Butterball in stretch pants: "Just pick it *up*!"

Dad: (yelling loudly) "Shut up! How *dare* you tell me to pick up? I *always* pick up!"

The butterball in stretch pants scurried away but Dad kept yelling.

Dad: "You won't tell the Mike *Tyson* look-a-like whose rottweiler just took a human-sized shit on your shoes to pick it up, will you? No! But you think you can yell at *me*, an old, white, *bald* man because you think I won't say anything, right? You think I'll be nice and scurry away with my little bag of shit. Well, you're *wrong*! And if you're so worried about how the neighborhood looks, why don't you knock a few pounds off that *ass*!"

Dad kills me. Mom was laughing because she grew up here and for her, yelling at people is a New York sport.

I really love New York. Everybody is very high energy—lots of yelling and complaining all over the place.

I'm going to make much more noise tomorrow morning in Central Park. I'll be very menacing and New Yawkish and have a *really* great time: "Shaddup!" "Up yours!" "Have a nice day, my ass!"

Katrina People Are Dumb and Mean

People are dumber and meaner than I thought.

I don't know how many animals died in the South this past week but I am disgusted with people because it's their fault. The hurricane was bad, sure. But these people who are running the "relief" operation are worse than a truckload of cat poop. They are telling people to abandon their pets and that the animals will be taken care of by the authorities. No one is taking care of anybody. People are dying and animals are dying horrible deaths right now because of a bunch of idiots.

Why can't they rescue *dogs*? Dogs rescue people *all the time*!

What is *wrong* with people?

And why would anybody leave a dog tied to a fence in the middle of a hurricane with water rising? Why can't the old lady be evacuated with her Seeing Eye dog?

What about the shelters? Why isn't there a single dog allowed in the shelters with his people? They let in rapists and criminals but they won't let in a single poodle or even a hamster.

My heart is broken from all of this. I know Mom and Dad wouldn't evacuate and leave us here to die. If there is ever a disaster here, we're not going to count on the government for anything. We're going to survive and if we don't, we're going to die together.

We're a pack.

16 September 2005

As Dumb as It Gets

My wife likes to play dress up in Mom's clothes. It's really sexy how it opens up right at her pee-pee. She looks smart in this photo but wait till you hear how dumb she is.

We discovered just how dumb Finn is this morning. It was early, before breakfast, and Finn was limping really badly around the garden. She was dragging her back leg and walking like she was going to spend the rest of her life in a stroller. Mom and Dad completely freaked out.

Mom: "Oh my God! Look at Finn! She's limping. Oh no!"

Dad: "That's it. That's how my old dog Kegley died. She tried to jump out of the car and her back went out."

Mom: "That's how my dachshund died! He became a paraplegic! Oh my God! Finn's going to be a paraplegic if she doesn't have surgery immediately! You have to do spinal surgery within twelve hours of the onset of paralysis or they are paralyzed for life!"

Then Mom helped Finley hobble up the steps from the pool to the bedroom. Mom and Dad helped her up onto the bed, where she plopped down. Mom and Dad were almost crying while they inspected her back legs and feet.

I knew there was nothing wrong with Finn other than extreme laziness, obesity, and general stupidity, but I hung around to watch the freak show at the foot of the bed. What an actress Finn is. A *fat* actress.

Finn allowed Dad to inspect her feet and he found a big, hard seed lodged in her foot pad.

Dad: "Oh, thank God. It's just a seed."

Mom: "What an idiot! She didn't even have the brains to shake her foot. It's like walking with a stone in your shoe! She didn't even *look* at her foot."

Dad: (in baby talk) "Oh dat Finney Finn! You're pretty dumb, dat Finney Finn. You didn't know there was something in your foot? Couldn't you look at your foot and take it out?"

Mom: "Well, we've now discovered the depths of her stupidity. She's a moron! Even Stupid Kitty would have shaken her foot to get the thing out. She shakes her feet when she gets out of her litter box. Jinky would have removed a stone in his footpad in a second."

I still love Finn even though she's dumb. She would probably *like* being paralyzed. Then she could just lie around wearing diapers in a stroller and get hand fed. I know none of this hysteria would have happened if there was a piece of *chicken* stuck in Finn's foot-pad. She would have gotten *that* out pronto.

19 September 2005

Emmy Meltdown and Hurricane Incompetence

Well, we suffered through another long night of Emmy baloney. I don't know how many more years I can take sitting in front of the TV watching a bunch of idiots congratulating themselves with gold statues for the "work" they do on television.

Like every year, none of these selfish humans thanked any of their dogs. None of these show biz phonies even *mentioned* that tens of thousands of animals might have died in Hurricane *Incompetence* (that's what I call Hurricane Katrina).

Actresses in ball gowns clutched their Emmys and tearfully pleaded with the audience to help those people down there in Mississippi and Louisiana but not one of them talked about the thousands of dogs and cats left there to drown or to die of starvation. These people make me want to throw up.

When the longest show on television was finally over, it was way past Minky Time (10:00 p.m.). Dad was depressed.

Dad: "Well, I'm officially out of the business! All those people are going to do better than me."

Mom: "That's not true."

Dad: "Yes it is, and I'm going to make *sure* of it."

Mom: "You're going to make sure that you don't do anything at all?"

Dad: "That's right, I don't have the talent. Nothing I write is funny."

Mom: "That's not true, you're very funny. You have talent, you just don't want to write anything."

Dad: "I can't write. I have nothing to say."

There are two Emmys with Dad's name on them just sitting on the shelf by the television and still, he finds a way to be depressed. Most people in this stupid town would kill for one of those silly gold statues. Dad uses one of them to flip burgers on the barbecue and he used the other one to smash a tape recorder in a fit of anger.

A show written by a writer Dad knows debuted last night and this morning, the numbers for the show were really bad, which is Hollywood speak for nobody watched it. For a while, Dad cheered up. The thing is, that's just a temporary happy feeling he's got, not real happiness. Real happiness comes from successfully chasing a squirrel completely out of my garden and scaring the poop out of a giant hawk who thinks he can come around here and drink the water out of my pool.

Dad Feels Alienated from Show Business

Dad had some wine in the garden with me and Finn. He felt good for a while (two glasses), then he sank like a rock (three glasses).

Dad: "I feel alienated from show business."

So Mom Photoshopped a picture of Dad and gave him a cone head with horns, making him look like an alien.

His feelings of alienation might have to do with the fact that his show got canceled and that since we

got back from Nice, France, Europe, he's gone on some pitch meetings and no one has called back.

In fact, the phone has hardly rung at all. After days of not ringing, it rang yesterday. Mom was Wi-Fi-ing by the pool and Dad was in the Jacuzzi making his lists about money in his notepad.

Mom: (jumping up out of her seat) "Oh my God, the phone is ringing. Did you bring it out?"

Dad: "What?"

Mom: "DID YOU BRING THE PHONE OUTSIDE WITH YOU WHEN YOU CAME OUT?"

Dad: "NO! DID YOU? Why are you yelling at me?"

I think they are both waiting for calls from their agents and managers. Mom went on an audition last week for the part of a Russian ballet dancer who teaches pro football players how to do amusing end zone dances. I saw Mom practicing her ballet and her Russian accent and I can't believe a show like that is actually getting made. But nothing surprises me in this town.

Mom went upstairs to check the answering machine. When she came back out to the garden she didn't look too happy.

Dad: "Who was it?"

Mom: "It was an automated call from BMW."

Rabbi Jinkleberg Quotes the Talmud

Our neighbors in the Hollywood Hills are "saving up to buy a poodle puppy." What a waste of money. Poodle puppies can cost over a thousand dollars. And by buying a dog, these nitwits are adding to the problem of pet overpopulation by giving money to jerks who breed more and more dogs who end up being homeless like I was.

"Love thy neighbor" is one of the Ten Commandments but that rule ought to be broken if your neighbor is an idiot. Here's why:

There are thousands of poodles (and every other kind of dog) who have been abandoned and who are sitting in the pound right now, waiting for someone to come and save them. If someone doesn't come and get them out of there now, they might get the lethal injection. I know they execute human criminals in some states, but none of my cell mates were criminals. They were all innocent. They were just nice dogs who were thrown away like garbage.

Celebrities who buy dogs as accessories should be squirted with cat pee. That Paris Hilton is such a dumbass. Why couldn't she take one of the million dogs who are on death row? Why don't these idiots just go to Petfinder.com? They can get any kind of purebred dog they're looking for. It's like a giant bargain bin on the Internet where you can find really good dogs. By the way, I've been to Paris. It's a classy place. Her name should be *Burbank* Hilton.

Don't the nitwits who buy puppies know about puppy mills? And that in a couple of months, the puppy turns into a dog anyway? I'm *way* cuter now than when I was a puppy. Ask Finley or any of the other bitches around Hollywood. Plus, when I was adopted, I was already past the puppy phase of chewing up Manolo Blahniks (those $700 spiked sandals Mom wore on *Sex and the City*).

The Talmud has a saying that could help a lot of dogs:

"If you save one life, it is as if you saved the whole world."

The Hills Are on Fire
and Bill Maher's Fart Doll

The hills all around us are on fire! The air is thick with smoke. The sky is bright orange and Burbank is burning. Animals are running for their lives and tens of thousands of acres are in flames.

Big planes full of water are flying over our house and thousands of birds are flying through the ashes, yelling to each other and freaking out. It smells like a giant barbecue but this time, it's not veggie burgers, it's *deer*.

Poised to rocket some gas

Usually, it's dumb-ass humans who start fires. Up here on Mulholland Drive, I've seen idiots driving giant Hummers and holding a burny stick out of the window. What do they think is going to happen if they're driving, talking on their cell, and flicking their ashes out the window? Maybe if their mansions burned down, they'd think about being a little more careful with their burny stinky sticks.

Speaking of burny stinky sticks, Mom, Dad, and a couple of their friends got into a fight last night with a group of loud, sequined chain smokers at a restaurant. All four of them had their stinky sticks burning at the same time, while we were eating.

Dad's friend is amazing. His name is David Feldman. He's a writer for Bill Maher and has funny hair on his head—kind of like the hair on the head of a doll, but that's not why he's so powerful. He has a Web site called DavidFeldmanisimpotent.com, but he's not at all, which I soon found out. Dad calls him Bill Maher's Fart Doll and now I understand why.

During dinner, Bill Maher's Fart Doll was sitting right next to the chain smokers and he was getting annoyed by the smoke.

Bill Maher's Fart Doll: (to the smoking lady sitting next to us) "Would you mind holding your cigarettes over *there*, not over here?"

Mom: (so they could hear) "Are they *allowed* to smoke here? This is LA! You can't even smoke at the beach in LA!"

Dad: "Well, we *are* outside. If he likes to smoke so much, I just wish that guy would blow the smoke on *his* guests, not *us*."

Chain smoker number one: (real phony) "Gee, I'm
    sorry. But we're outside here, aren't we?"

Bill Maher's Fart Doll: "OK, I'm going to ask you
    politely one more time. Either hold your
    cigarettes on your side of the table or put
    them out. My wife has asthma. I'm not going to
    ask you again."

    Then the other two people at their table lit more
cigarettes, completely ignoring Fart Doll. They
laughed at us and blew more smoke our way.

Mrs. Fart Doll: (to Fart Doll) "Honey, are you carry-
    ing? Are you loaded?"

Bill Maher's Fart Doll: (to Mrs. Fart Doll) "I'll
    take care of this."

    Then the most incredible thing happened. FD stood
up very calmly, lifted up his jacket, positioned
himself with his ass directly in front of one of the
chain smokers and blew a high-pressure gas bomb right
in her face, giving her an instant chemical peel!
    Her sequins melted.
    The Fart Doll's gas was *so* powerful, a cloud of
vapors hovered over the chain smokers and they started
choking from the fumes. They looked like they were
about to die. FD claims he's a vegetarian but he's
lying. I know that gas had some pork fat and cheese
pushing its way through the tube of raw sewage before
it shot out of his khakis.
    He must be the most powerful man in Hollywood. If
he worked for the government, that would be the end

of all wars. They could harvest that ass gas of his and attach it to long-range missiles. That's the only shortfall of his weapon. He doesn't have the long-range delivery power.

I might be able to help him with that. It's something to work on. A viable Hollywood project. Bill Maher should let his Fart Doll loose on his show. It would blow away the competition.

Schadenfreude

Stupid Kitty taunting coyotes

Stupid Kitty has no idea that the even stupider kitty down the street was found in several pieces last week after a meeting with a coyote. Mom hardly ever lets her come out unless she's on a leash but when Stupid Kitty does come out, she's really happy about being able to stink up the garden furniture and maybe get a chance to kill something. Sometimes, she'll get lucky and catch a really dumb, slow fly that's too stupid to move. This makes her happy.

I don't want her to get eaten or anything like that, but I'd sure like to see a big fat crow swoop down and poop on her head. It would be so cool to watch a nice flyby and guano-drop right between those creepy nonblinking eyes of hers.

Dad calls that "schadenfreude," that great feeling you get when something lousy happens to somebody else. It's Dad's favorite thing, I think. Like today, he was *dancing* because someone he knows had a bad box office weekend gross. (That's the pile of dough that a movie makes opening weekend and if it doesn't do well in the first two days, the movie dies.)

Mom was looking up the "opening weekend numbers" on some dumb movie and it had bombed. Dad was so happy! You'd think he had just found a pile of money because he was twirling around and pumping his middle finger in the air just because the movie had flopped.

Dad: "Ha ha! Hee hee! Ha ha ha ha ha! That's what you get, you didn't want to consult *me* about making it funny! 'Cause I'm old. The old bald man. That's what you get when you put out movies with the *young* sensibility, the kind of movie that's *hip* and in touch with what *young* people want to see, huh? Penis and snot jokes, right, Jinky? By next week, it'll disappear, you pompous, superior melon head. Hee ha hee!"

Mom: "I *read* for that movie! He could have hired me and at least had one funny scene, but no! Wow. What a bomb! All bad reviews. Did you see? All Ds and Fs."

Dad: "I hate critics unless they hate something I hate and then the morons are all geniuses. Hee hee hee."

Then the Yankees lost and Mom and Dad were delirious. They were having a real schadenfreude night. They were jumping up and down and dancing. *Dancing* because a team *lost*!

Mom: (screaming out over the balcony so the whole canyon could hear her) "Whoooooooooo! Woooooooooooo ooeeeeeeeeeeeee!"

Dad: "OK, OK, that's enough! Can't tempt karma. Remember when I got all excited when Dennis Miller's show got canceled and a day later *my* show got canceled?"

15 October 2005

The Worst Fall Foliage Season in History

We've been on a road trip through New Hampshire, Maine, and Massachusetts in the second-worst weather in recorded history. I hate to think what the *worst* weather in recorded history was like because this has been *bad*. *Really* bad. Dangerous bad, with flooding rivers, dead bodies, washed-out roads, and none of what we came here for . . . foliage.

Even though it's all soggy, I still love this road trip. The air is so clean; you can smell a moose poop hundreds of miles away. There are tons of animals who live here that don't live in Hollywood, like tiny, striped chipmunks, who dart around the trees. Finley looks like she woke up out of a coma here. She's all worked up about running through dead leaves and finding something alive to chase.

Of course, Mom and Dad have been complaining nonstop. They've been fighting like they were in the Octagon cage (the "Extreme Fighting" you see on pay-per-view) except that this cage is a gray rented Grand Am with zero horsepower.

Everyone we meet says it's the worst fall foliage season in history and that there's no "cuhlah" (that's how they pronounce "color" ovah heah). But I've seen plenty of cuhlah. I saw a bright red bird and all the New England humans wear red, orange, or bright green stretchy outfits.

The New England humans look like a different species than the humans in Hollywood or Paris. They smell different too. They're not doused with perfume and the females don't wear as much makeup or high spiky shoes. There's no weird, expressionless BOTOX look here and the lady human lips don't look like huge jelly donuts, stuffed with their own ass fat. The human males here all look like they could build stuff. In LA, the human males look all like manicured poodles.

Even the *dogs* in New England are bigger and tougher looking. And the dogs here *work*.

Dad has some land in New Hampshire that he inherited. Since Dad grew up here, he thought it might be great to come home and he wanted to show Mom, hoping that she would like it enough to move here. But I don't think that's going to happen.

Dad: "All my dreams about living here are dead. Dead as the leaves we're driving through. You can't go home again . . . but in my case it's because of the food. Miles and miles of Dunkin' Donuts and fatties in flannel shirts. You can't even get a latte here—they look at you like you're nuts. 'Latte? What's *that*?' They don't want to change *anything*. It's just like I remember. All shitty little houses. Except now it costs $5 million to live on a swamp called 'Lake' Winnipesauke and get devoured by mosquitoes, gnats, and black flies."

Mom: "Yeah, and there's nothing fresh here! At the store, all they have is apples and iceberg lettuce! I'd never be able to cook anything I like here! And look at all the NO HUNTING signs everywhere. That means they're hunting and murdering animals all over the place! All the hotels have giant stuffed, decapitated moose heads. We are deep in the heartless land."

Dad: "It *is* beautiful, though, don't you think? All these tall trees? You don't see anything like that in LA."

Mom: "No, we have *palm* trees in LA."

Dad: "Palm trees are phony, ridiculous trees. They're not real trees. It's a giant bush with a rat in it. They're ugly. They belong in Baghdad."

Mom: "In LA, we have lush vegetation and we can buy
snow peas and porcini mushrooms. There are flowers
everywhere. You stick something in the ground in
California and it *grows*. Here, if you don't up-
root everything every year and bring it indoors,
it *dies* in the freezing cold. And it gets dark at
four in the afternoon and you wake up in the *dark*
half the year. I'll kill myself here in the land
of fatties in flannel who hunt."

I'm telling you, all they did was fight in the car.
It rained for a week straight and we were lost almost
the whole time. Neither one of them knows how to read
a map and Dad was too cheap to get the GPS system op-
tion from Avis.

Mom: "Where are we going to eat? We haven't seen
anything but McDonald's and Dunkin' Donuts for
hours! We're running out of gas, you know."

Then, through the fog, we saw a place in the White
Mountains that served live "lawbstah" (that's how they
say "lobster" up heah). Dad wanted to stop there so he
could get some clam chowdah. I don't get it. How do
all those lawbstahs get up to the mountains? There are
no lawbstahs living anywhere *near* here. I can't understand how anybody would want to eat a thing like that.
Don't get me wrong, I love meat, like Dad. And I would
kill to get it if I was living alone in the woods, but
a lawbstah? And clams just look like the things that
come flying out of Stupid Kitty's nose. Ew.

Mom: "How awful. They must bring all these lobsters
from the coast, *alive*, knowing they're going

to be boiled *alive* and eaten by these horrible people with hunting rifles wearing red flannel. I can't go in there. I can't look at them alive in the tank like that. If I try to liberate them, I'll get arrested for domestic terrorism."

Dad: "I'm going to get some fried clams to go, then."

Then we got stuck on a washed-out road while Dad ate his fried kitty snots.

Live Free or Die

We finally found our hotel, the Motel Moose. The people here are cozy, flannel-wearing dog lovers. We have a big cabin with couches and beds and there is a kitchen. It's a fantastic place, completely surrounded by woods, very few people, and lots of wild animals, even bears. But as usual, my people are complaining again. They're never satisfied.

Mom: "Oh my God. Look at these silly curtains. They've got ruffles and pom-poms. Can you imagine having this beautiful view of the woods and hiding it with polyester ruffles?"

Dad: "Yup, it's all pretty corny up here in winky world. It's sad to come back here and realize that everything I thought was good was really shit. Let's go to dinner."

Mom: "What the hell would I *wear* here? There's no glamour."

They got really hungry from all the criticizing, so we all walked to the village for dinner.
As soon as they got served, it started again.

Mom: "Yuck! My butternut squash soup is full of sugar! They made it with maple syrup. Can you believe it? And to top it off, they put a fried apple fritter covered in *sugar* floating in it. I can't eat this, it's poison."

Dad: "This is supposed to be the best restaurant in town. My fish is like a dried-up brick. I don't know what they did to it."

Mom: "If I'm going to be this far from a city, I want to at *least* see a live moose."

Dad: "You did—the waitress who just served your maple syrup soup."

The next morning, we drove to the coast and Finley and I ran on the big, wide beach at Ogunquit, Maine. It was the greatest beach I ever ran on. Unbelievable traction, world-class seagull chasing, perfect sand consistency, and cool, breezy salt air.

I felt like a big, strong, Northeast beast—like I could jump as high as the sky.

It might be the worst fall foliage season in history, but I *love* New England. There's no pollution, the water in the creeks is crystal clear and delicious, and the people aren't phony show business dummies.

What they say in New Hampshire makes a lot of sense to someone like me, having done time on death row. "Live free or die."

Finley the French Maid
Goes to a Halloween Party

Finley: "Is your house dirty? I'll make it *filthy!*"

Mom got us all dressed up and dragged us to Bow Wow Ween, a Hollywood dog costume party in Brentwood. It was supposed to be for a good cause—to benefit homeless dogs (Much Love and other adoption orgs were there) but I got into some fights.

Mom: "Oh no! We've got to get him outta here, he's biting everybody!"

Dad: "I told you he needs a muzzle but you won't listen to me."

The winner of the grand prize at Bow Wow Ween—a hermit crab. He pulled his crab float around all day. Finley tried to kill the crab because it won.

I might have been bad but Finley didn't act like a lady either. She knew it wasn't merely a costume party, she knew it was a *contest*. Finn doesn't like to lose. She was attacking all the contestants and we had to pull her out of there because she was so aggressive in her little maid outfit. She wanted to win, eat everybody's food, and intimidate the competition, so we had to leave.

As we were walking toward the parking lot, we passed a lot of nutty-looking people coming in to enter their dogs in the contest.

Neurotic dog nut number one: "Oh, look at the cute French maid! It's a French maid!"

Neurotic dog nut number two: "Look at the adorable French maid shitting in the parking lot! Aw, she's so cute, the French maid!"

I think we ruined Mom's day.
We were bad.

Pompous Melon Head (P.M.)

Oops, P.M. (Pompous Melon Head) found my blog,
hollywooddog.blogspot.com.

Remember the day that Mom and Dad were having
that typically Hollywood schadenfreude moment—
when they were ecstatic that a dumb-ass movie had
bombed? Well, P.M. found out and got all freaked
out about it.

The P.M. "*writer/director*" wrote me a totally
whiny e-mail about his movie and how it's going to
break even in DVD sales.

I might have been a little more interested if he
wrote to me about a squirrel party at his house up
the street instead of carrying on and on about his
movie . . . again.

P.M. then continued to preach and moan to me about
what Mom ought to know about movies and nap-provoking
details about how film financing works, which is *really*
weird because Mom's made a *lot* more movies than he
has—with *real* directors and *real* writers.

Mom and Dad aren't mean people. They saved me. But
they do go bananas when ass-burning, unfunny movies
or TV shows get hyped up in Hollywood.

Mom never meant to hurt P.M.'s feelings. She sent
him a bottle of vodka and a letter explaining that
her glee hadn't been about *his particular* movie fail-
ing, that it was all in good fun, and that she and
Dad had indulged privately in a bit of nasty merri-
ment, hoping that he would leave it at that.

But P.M. wouldn't let it go. He accused her of

lying and he threatened to cut us off of his Christmas card list.

I barely know the P.M., but whenever we run into this dude in the street, all he talks about is himself and his *movie*. The way he gasses on and on about being a "writer/director," you would think he was making *Old Yeller* (now *that* was a movie) but all he was doing was making a gross-out video for teenage boys.

You know what's really even grosser than his movie? For two weeks, P.M. had a sewage leak streaming out of his house and pouring down our street, right to our front gate. I had to step over it on my walks. He was so busy talking about his *movie* all the time, it never occurred to him that it might be dangerous for us to be exposed to that much . . . liquid Hollywood poop.

He's since fixed it, but man, the stench was unforgettable. You know what's funny? His liquid poop had a longer run than his movie.

Me and Dad watching the trailer to P.M.'s movie

Breadwinner

I'm the breadwinner of the pack now. I got a book deal!

I feel sorry for Mom and Dad because my career is taking off and both of their careers are buried like an old bone. Neither one of them is making any money so I'm going to have to take care of them.

I got a small advance and I'm going to get a publicist to maximize sales because we've got a lot of bills around here. Mom and Dad are going to have to cut down on their spending habits, like shopping for silly stuff they don't need. It's kind of weird between me and Dad because *he* wanted to be the one who had a book out and here I am, a *dog*, and I've got a publisher.

I explained to Finn that I'm not going to do the Hollywood thing and dump her for a younger, hotter bitch.

A really close friend of mine, Mark Brazill, the guy who created *That '70s Show*, is bringing my project to Universal to see if they want to develop a series for me. This is killing Mom.

Mom: "I can't *believe* it—Jinky's going to get a series and I'll have to audition to play his mom! And then they won't give it to me. I won't even be able to play *myself*. They'll want to go younger!"

Dad: "Maybe you can get a small part in it."

Mom: "I hope at least you'd get to write on it."

Dad: "The best I could do is get hired to do punch up. And I bet if I thought up a line for my character, some pinhead network guy would tell me 'I don't think he'd say that.' And I'd say, but he's *me*. Are you telling me I don't know what I'd say? Then the network guy would say 'Well, he *is* you, but younger.' So you're saying . . . I can't remember what I've said?"

Mom: "You know what? They'll probably want a store-bought, purebred dog to play Jinky."

Dad: "Jinky can't play himself. He'll bite the network people. He's the only honest guy in Hollywood."

I don't care if they get a real actor to play me because the important thing is that my story gets told so I can help my old cell mates and get them out of the shelter.

Chinese Hairless Pervs

I did *not* have sexual relations with that dog and this has got nothing to do with my book deal.

That Chinese hairless guy came over again and this time, he brought his perverted cousin.

I don't know how it happened, but I got sucked into a ménage situation. I'm not proud of it and I swear, I didn't touch that guy, but Finn was pretty close to his winky—talking right into the microphone, you know what I mean? It was wrong.

I feel kind of weird. I think I might need therapy.

The older one just likes to watch his cousin party while he pees all over his T-shirt.

The Chinese hairless guys wouldn't leave. They stayed for dinner and hogged all the people food.

Their mom is a famous TV actress and she talks to them like they're nuclear physicists.

Hairless perv's mom: "Stanley, please can you find a way to come back here because you've gone off a little too far. . . . Thank you, Stanley. I appreciate it. Thank you. I just prefer you stay in the vicinity. Thank you very much, Stanley."

Mom: "Do you take them to India when you go?"

Hairless perv's mom: "Of course. They go to the ashram and meditate. Arnold is in an *advanced* state of meditation. He's a very old soul and he might even be the reincarnation of an important peaceful energy that is going to change the world as we know it."

Then Arnold, who was sitting on Dad's lap, slipped him the tongue! He slipped his long, slimy tongue right into Dad's mouth. I'm telling you, these guys are not in any advanced stage of meditation. They're in an advanced state of *mas*turbation, maybe. They have Dad completely fooled. They are totally debauched. Dad just sat there making goo-goo eyes at a Chinese pervert with pimples.

Dad: "Look how cute he is! He *likes* me! . . . Is this a mole? What is this on his neck?"

Hairless perv's mom: "Oh that's just a zit. It's nothing. He has sensitive skin."

Ew.

Mom: "Your dog has zits?"

Hairless perv's mom: "We have a great dermatologist in Beverly Hills. He's going next week."

Mom: "Your derm sees dogs?"

Hairless perv's mom: "No, no, no, no. He just sees *this* dog. As a favor to me. I've sent every actress in Hollywood to him."

Meanwhile, Stanley was bouncing off the walls, screaming, running around on his hind legs, and ripping apart everything we own. He peed on Mom's Persian carpet. At one point, he got so out of control, Finley tried to kick his ass.

Scared off by Finn, Stanley ran downstairs to do things to Stupid Kitty.

I hope he holds her down in the new igloo litter box and really lets her have it.

16 November 2005

We're Fired!

Demonic, evil, scurrilous, and bad

We got fired by our housekeeper.

Our house is pretty grimy. At the end of the week, we've got food, dog and cat hair, puked-up left-overs, and mud caked into the floorboards. The beds and couches all need a good airing out and piles of underwear and socks litter the bedroom.

That's when Gaspara comes over. But she's not going to come over anymore because she hates Mom. She hates Mom because Mom doesn't go to church every day and because of the books Mom has on the coffee table. Gaspara won't dust the coffee table until Mom removes certain books. The books are: *Sex Lives of the Popes* and *The Devil: A Visual Guide to the Demonic, Evil, Scurrilous, and Bad.* Gaspara wants to burn the books in the fireplace.

Mom thinks these books are fun and informative and that the house can be cleaned for $20 an hour without being harassed by a grand inquisitor with a dust mop. Gaspara wants Mom to burn in hell.

Mom believes in tolerance and she thinks people should believe whatever they want. I believe in Santa Claus and Mom doesn't, but that doesn't cause any problems between us at Christmas. I also believe in the tooth fairy and look forward to losing my teeth when I get older so I can find treats under the pillow. But Gaspara is always trying to convert Mom.

Mom: (gently) "Gaspara, we have to talk about all the bleach you always put in the dark wash load. The bleach is for the white stuff, OK?"

Gaspara: "What are joo doing for Easter this jeer?"

Mom: "You ask me this every year, Gaspara. I'm doing exactly what you do for Passover—*nothing.*"

Gaspara fired us the next day. I'm glad she fired us. She didn't like me or Finley or Stupid Kitty. She would always look at me from the corner of her eye like she wanted me to drop dead.

We got a new housekeeper now who doesn't care what Mom reads and she likes me and Finley. And we like Pepita.

Fired from Hollywood

First Gaspara fired us and now I think we've been fired by Hollywood because Mom and Dad were bad. Well, Dad was bad. Mom is just old.

Dad completely forgot he had a meeting. He was a no-show with the head of reality programming at some network. While we were getting waterlogged in the Jacuzzi, Dad's agent called.

Dad's agent: "What are you doing?"

Dad: "Oh, just having a glass of wine in the Jacuzzi with my Minky."

Dad's agent: "Your *Minky?* What's a Minky?"

Dad: "My dog, Minky . . . Stinky, Minky, Jinky. We're having a glass of vino here in the hot tub. (To me) Right, Jinky?"

Dad's agent: "What are you doing!? You had a meeting you were supposed to go to! They're calling to find out what happened!"

Dad: (laughing) "Oh, Christ. I forgot . . . agh, they're not going to do a show with me anyway. I'm just a preholiday schedule filler."

Dad's agent: "Do you want me to reschedule it?"

Dad: "Not really. Right, Minky?"

Dad's agent: "I guess you can have that attitude if you have screw-you money."

Dad: "I don't have screw-you money. But I do have screw-*me* money. Meaning, I suppose I should reschedule but 'screw me,' I'm staying here with my Minky."

Mom's not doing much better than Dad. She had a preholiday audition for a show called *Cold Case* and she's really depressed about it because the name of the role is "Old Sloane." Apparently, this show is

about young criminals and old witnesses and guess
what Mom would play.

So Mom went and read for the old role and she got
called back for producers. Callbacks are hard on Mom
because she always gets the same feedback.

Mom's agent: "They *loved* you but they are going
     another way."

Mom: "You know what? I've had enough rejection this
     year. *I'm* going another way . . . to the south
     of France."

Then Mom and Dad made plane reservations for us to
leave Hollywood and go back to Nice, France, Europe, so
that they won't kill themselves this holiday season.

They are so spoiled. If they only knew how lucky
they are.

Christmas in Nice, France, Europe

It's holiday season in Nice, France, Europe, and the palm trees lining the Promenade des Anglais (the main drag on the beach) are wrapped up in lights. The French dogs are all dressed up in crazy outfits and the smells of delicious Christmas food are floating out of every window.

Mom and I went to the outdoor market to get some *salade* and while Mom was talking to the vegetable man about some tomatoes, the butcher from the next stand got all excited and called out to Mom.

French butcher: "Madame! Eeeeet's been so long!
Deeeeed you leave your husband in America zeees

time? I hope so. Look! I 'ave some fantastique farming cheeeeckens for you!"

The butcher was shaking a chicken at Mom and she was horrified. The head on the chicken had all of its feathers and its crown so it looked like it was just sleeping. The butcher kept shaking the dead chicken, making its head flop around while he was flirting with Mom. . . . He was literally choking his chicken.

Mom: "Yes, my husband is here in France. And *please*, would you not shake the poor thing in my face? Don't show me the chicken! I'm very sensitive! That poor thing—no, I'm just here for some salad next door."

French butcher: "Ah! On top of your beauty, you are sensitive, too? Don't tell your husband but I will never forget that time I saw you at zee flower market downtown and you were wearing a blue summer dress and carrying a basket of roses. Ah . . . you were a vision. Please! Let me give you some meat, I insist."

Mom: "No thank you. I just want vegetables. Good day, Monsieur. The bloody apron is a real turn-on, though."

When we got home, Dad surprised us with a Christmas tree. The tree looked more like a shrub, and Mom thought it was puny for the gigantic living room.

Mom: "Look at it. It looks ridiculous! It's a chiseler's tree, a dwarf tree, a cheapo tree. We should have gotten a bigger tree for this room."

Dad: "Well, that's all the Christmas we're going to get. You got an apartment in France. That should hold you over for a couple of Christmases, I hope."

Mom: "You're so Bah Humbuggish. Oh well, I'll get some cute balls and we'll decorate it the best we can. (Really sarcastic) Don't worry, I'll go to the *cheap* store and get the smallest balls I can find."

Then Mom, Finley, and I went out again in search of tiny silver balls to hang on the mini-tree and we found a cheap, stuffed Santa for 1 euro.

As soon as we got home, Finley got ahold of Santa and ripped him to shreds. All that was left of him was his head.

Dad: (holding up the decapitated Santa head) "Look! It's Merry Christmas from Al-Qaeda!"

Then Dad pulled his black turtleneck over his face like a terrorist and put on a bin Laden accent.

Dad: "No more Santa for you! We have cut off his head. Santa is the infidel son of pigs and dogs!"

Why do those terrorist guys always call us Americans "sons of dogs"? Dogs aren't so bad, you know. I can understand why Dad isn't so gung ho about Christmas. I've always believed in Santa but lately I've got a problem with Santa that's been bothering me. Why does Santa give way more stuff to rich people? I mean he's supposed to give you stuff if you're *nice*, not rich.

Crappy New Year

It's New Year's Eve and Mom and Dad can't figure out what to wear. Mom wants to look nice *and* hot. So she's now tried on about a thousand different outfits trying to look like both of those things and nothing is working.

Dad's actually going to change. He's going to finally take off his Euro-exercise outfit, a sleeveless number that is the exact same color as his skin . . . pink.

Dad: "I'm going to wear the green plaid jacket."

Mom: "Oh, I *love* that jacket. You look so handsome and Irish in it."

Then Dad started to shave while Finley barked her head off at the firecrackers and I tried to nap.

Dad: "It's been ten years since my dad died, ten years that I've had diabetes. I haven't exercised in ten years and I'm a worthless schmuck."

Mom: (painting her face in the mirror) "You have such a low opinion of yourself; you must think I'm *really* worthless, then. I'm just your tick."

Dad: "No, you're a woman. That's a five-letter word for tick."

Mom: "That's nice for New Year's Eve. I'm your tick. Thanks a lot."

Dad: (wiping the rest of the shaving cream off his face) "I'm just lucky some dumber people than me gave me a lot of money. Money made by people smarter than both of us."

Mom: "So you're a worthless schmuck and I'm your tick."

Dad: "That's right, I'm a piece of shit with a lot of money and you're the tick that feeds off me."

Mom: "Well, happy New Year to you, too."

Herpe-wood

We got some very disturbing news about Zelda, who stayed in Hollywood while we are in Nice, France, Europe. Stupid Kitty doesn't like to fly with luggage and Mom and Dad are only allowed to carry one animal each on the plane, so she stayed in Hollywood with some friends.

These friends of hers are four old and debauched cats who live with a human who calls herself "The Pissed Kitty."

So Stupid Kitty has been hanging around Pissed Kitty's party house and really raising hell over there. She's been dancing and getting high nonstop, supposedly.

Now listen to this: There is an outbreak of kitty herpes at the Hollywood party house and several kitties now have herpes, including STUPID KITTY!

Stupid Kitty has allegedly been such a party ani-

mal that she is now being blamed for bringing a shameful venereal disease upon the Hollywood party house of Pissed Kitty.

Pissed Kitty claims it had to be Stupid Kitty's fault because her cats "never go out." Right. Like I

Photo by Rachel Riskind

believe *that*. But even if they aren't trolling outside, it's not like they don't have a bunch of wild
parties over there all the time . . . inside. God
only knows what kind of diseased and drunken street
cats climb over the balcony and crawl through a crack
in the wall to get a load of the steamy goings-on in
that joint.

Mom has offered to pay the vet bills for all of
Pissed Kitty's kitties and to rid them of this dread-
ful and shameful plague, but there is nothing she can
do about their reputations! They have *herpes*!

Ew.

I don't know how I will face her when we go home
to Hollywood.

It's Feudal to Resist

Though we are thousands of miles away, Nice, France, Europe, is getting to be a little like the set of that old movie *Sunset Boulevard*. I think both Mom and Dad are as they say . . . ready for their close-up.

They've now set up dog beds in the fireplaces. Since it's warm in the south of France, they don't make fires in the fireplaces; they make dog beds. All the fireplaces in the apartment are stuffed with pillows covered with blankets. We're supposed to sit in

them, like burning logs and pose for pictures. Weird.

I hope Santa doesn't come down off-season and kill us by mistake.

Dad is still depressed about not investing in Google and so he looks at stock charts all day counting how much money he could have made.

Dad: "Sigh . . . "

Mom: "What's wrong *now*?"

Dad: "Oh, nothing. If only I had had the *balls* to put some money in Google. But when the market opens, I'm too busy doing millions of chores."

Mom: "Blame *me* for going to the hardware store exactly at opening bell, why don't you. What about eBay? That's a good company and it's exploding in Europe."

Dad: "Too late. It's just hovering."

Mom: "Why don't you write something? You could sell it."

I tried to cheer Dad up by jumping on his lap.

Dad: "I can see now that I'm never going to write anything. I'm fifty-five years old and soon I'm going to be dead. Hi, Minky!"

Then Dad got out the camera, put on some crazy rave music, and took tons of pictures of Mom wearing fishnet stockings on the new Japanese bed. I posed, too.

Dad: "Ooh . . . you look great."

Mom: "Who, me?"

Dad: "No, Jinky."

You would think that Mom and Dad were going to do that crazy naked wrestling thing they do but Dad went back to his stock charts and then to bed at 9:30, a half hour before Minky Time (10:00 p.m.). He put the covers over his head and snored.

La Grippe Aviaire/French Birdy Flu

Birdy flu has arrived in France. Not in Nice . . .
yet. But Mom is pushing it by making goo-goo eyes at
a birdy that lives on a TV antenna outside our apartment. The birdy flies all around the apartment looking for Mom all day long, waiting for her to give him
some wild bird seeds. She's actually *buying* food for
this birdy and talking to it. I don't like it.

Mom: (to her birdy-boyfriend) "I don't understand
      why anyone would keep a bird like you in a cage.
      It's like prison!"

Last night on the news, they were talking about how we should all stay away from wild birdies because they might have *la Grippe Aviaire* (Birdy Flu) and if we see a dead birdy, we should call the *Département d'Agriculture* immediately.

I don't speak French, so I can't complain to the *Département d'Agriculture*, but every time that wild birdy comes to the window, which is like a thousand times a day, I run to the window to chase it.

Dad: "Jinky! Go get that birdy!"

Mom: "No, Jinky! Leave my birdy alone! That's *my* birdy! He's my little friend! He's a Eurasian Ring-Necked Dove and he likes me. And don't encourage Jinky to go after birds. It's not nice."

Nice? He's not nice . . . he's greedy, that's all. He comes around looking to take advantage of Mom. They're saying 140 million people are gonna die from this birdy flu!

Mom: "I think he's trying to mate with me! Look! He's bowing and showing me his feathers and dancing and cooing to me! I think we're in love!"

I've got to convince Mom that this friendship of hers with that incredibly *greedy* birdy could end badly. She's trying to train it to fly into her hand! I'll show that birdy something far worse than birdy flu, I will. He won't have time to get birdy flu around me. It'll be quick. Then those French Agriculture people can come over here and see what happened. I'll get rid of every bird in France *before* the birdy flu gets 'em. I'll save all of Europe . . . and my mom.

Mom: "Bird flu is so sad. All the chickens in France have to stay indoors now. That's the only life they have before they end up on a plate."

Dad: "Sigh . . . "

Mom: "What *now*? Still depressed about not investing in Google? They say the stock is going to lose 50 percent. That might be a buying dip."

Dad: "No. We're all going to get bird flu. We'll be dead soon. The housing market will collapse and this place will be worth nothing."

Why can't there be some kind of *Mean* Person Flu, like meany-flu, where only mean people get sick and give it to other mean people? There are at least 140 million mean people in this world, like the ones who bought me and beat me up before I got adopted by Mom and Dad.

There is so much hysteria here about the riots and the birdy flu that Mom and Dad have made reservations to fly back to Hollywood. No matter where they fly, they can't escape themselves.

Mom's new birdy-boyfriend

Couturophobia

The knitting project manager needs Zoloft.
Look at my mom. She's lost it.

We haven't even been back in Hollywood for two weeks and things are already going downhill. Mom had an audition for a show called *Ugly Betty* and once again, "they *loved* her but are going another way."

This book about me that's coming out has seriously changed the dynamics in the household. It's getting out of hand. The publisher has sent me some money and now I am officially making more money than my parents. This has destroyed Dad, who used to be the one bringing home the dough. Mom is taking it OK. . . . She's used to it now.

My book, *The Diary of Jinky: Dog of a Hollywood Wife*, is being released and Mom has created a line of sweaters for me that she is going to sell to "high-end Hollywood boutiques." I'm worried about her, though, as she frantically knits all these sweaters for the Mommy and Doggie line.

Personally, I think the whole thing is ridiculous and I'm not sure we look good wearing the same clothes. I'm already ball-less. So now I have no balls and I'm wearing the same purple sweater as my mommy. It's not exactly masculine.

This morning over coffee, I was trying to nap in her lap while she talked to her manufacturer in Canada.

Mom: "I think there's a niche market of spoiled, rich, Hollywood people who will splurge for a one-of-a-kind dog sweater. But it's got to be a hip, rock 'n' roll, Hollywood, Paris, Milan kind of vibe. Like Dolce, but for dogs."

I hope she outsources the knitting because I can't even sit on her lap when she knits. I'll get my eye poked out with a knitting needle. I'll be blind for my book tour.

Dad thinks the whole idea is crazy.

Dad: (yelling) "What the hell do you know about the clothing business? This is *crazy*! Do you want a bunch of people in the game room knitting and boxes piled up to the ceiling? What about the shipping? You want to be shipping this junk all over the place? What a headache! What if somebody is knitting and falls down the stairs or

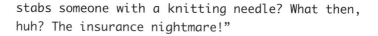

stabs someone with a knitting needle? What then, huh? The insurance nightmare!"

Mom: "I think this is an opportunity to help dogs. If this goes, we can give a part of the money to dog charities! *And* it's an opportunity to hire older women who knit . . . who *need* money! Old women can't get jobs, you know."

Dad: "Great. A bunch of old ladies and illegal aliens in my house. I used to have parties here. Now I've got a sweatshop!"

Mom: "Jesus! Do you always have to be so negative?"

Dad: "Well, blindfold 'em before you bring them up here. I don't want them to know where I live."

I'd much rather Mom got into the catering business.

The Over-40 Death March

Photo by Maximilian Canepa

Mom's giving Hollywood one last chance before she begs Dad to sell the house and moves us all to a farmhouse in Tuscany.

This week has been a major effort. I went with her to edit her new "speed reel," a one-minute video extravaganza of lots of different TV shows Mom worked on. The problem with her new reel is that all the shows on it have been canceled. So now,

Hollywood producers can click on a thumbnail of Mom on the Internet and watch her in action on canceled shows.

But they're not clicking on Mom. They're clicking on *me*. I've got a Web page on MySpace.com now and hundreds of people are adding me as their friend. MySpace.com is a ridiculous place on the Internet where a hundred million people and dogs are supposedly making "friends." These so-called friends are a lot like Hollywood friends. And Hollywood friends are like fleas. They jump around a lot to get attention and then they suck the blood out of you.

Hollywood is harsh. You're only as good as what you're working on right *now*. Even if you were working on something a month ago, that's old news, and if you're not actually working on a show today, you're like a stray dog, covered in the stink of loserdom.

Mom is six and a half in dog years and that's old in Hollywood. Even when there is a role for a six-and-a-half-year-old actress, like on Heather Locklear's new show, *Women of a Certain Age*, Mom can't catch a break. She studied her lines all night and this morning, she spent hours rehearsing and doing her hair when her manager called.

Mom's manager: "Honey, they cut the role from the script. I'm sorry."

Mom: "What?! I was just leaving for Disney in Burbank! This is so depressing."

No, Mom. Darfur is depressing. Famine is depressing. Dogs getting tortured in laboratories is depressing. Not getting a Disney pilot is not what I would call depressing. Actresses. Sometimes you just want to bite them in the ass.

But Mom just stood there, motionless in the gar-den—in disbelief, hands in the air like an Iraqi bomb victim.

For old actresses, Hollywood is a war zone, like Baghdad. Unseen forces are always trying to kill your career, and every audition is a roadside bomb.

We might have to pull out.

What If I Bite Kim Basinger?

I've got six more days until I get in the ring at the big "Nuts for Mutts" Dog Show. It's a fund-raiser for homeless dogs and a spoof of the Westminster Dog Show. None of the dogs have pedigrees. All the bitches have been spayed, which doesn't matter 'cause none of the guy dogs even have *balls.* It's kind of like the Democratic Party.

I feel a lot of pressure because Mom really wants me to win. I don't know what it's going to be like there, all the way out in Woodland Hills in the heat with hundreds of mutts competing for Best in Show. We're going to be climbing over mountains of dog poop. I'm in the Terrier Mix group and I have to run around a ring with Mom to see if I even qualify.

I've been boiling myself in the Jacuzzi and getting mentally prepared for a big, phony Hollywood letdown.

Mom: "He'd better qualify."

Dad: "What if he bites the judges?"

Mom: "It's being hosted by Kim Basinger. She'd better not try to touch him or he'll bite her."

Dad: "What if we're like those parents who think their kid is a genius and then as soon as he gets into a school they find out their kid is retarded—that the kid is the dumbest kid in the class?"

Mom: "That's not possible. He's the smartest and no one is cuter."

Dad: "What if it's all rigged, like everything else in this town?"

Mom: "Don't be so negative. He's going to *win*. He *has* to win."

Mom is acting like a hyper-caffeinated stage mother. Just because she can't get an acting job in this town, does it mean that I have to be put through the anxiety of having to be cuter than every other dog?

We looked on the Internet to see how the show went last year. Other than Kim Basinger, most of the celebrities were definitely B-list, like Mom. Eric Roberts was there. Mom played his wife on that *Less Than Perfect* show that got canceled. He's a really nice guy and I hope he's there this year because in Hollywood, it's all about who you know.

Mom and Dad have been squabbling over who gets to parade me in front of the judges. The Barbie Twins (those calendar girls with gigantic boobs) are supposed to judge this year. When they show up together, they look like a watermelon truck in a blond wig. I think it's totally bogus that the Barbie Twins get to decide if I'm cute enough to win. Ken Wahl, the old *Wiseguy* from TV, might be on the panel. He used to be married to Mom's best friend and doesn't like Mom very much. So I'm sure he'll be giving me the fish-eye. I think it's totally bogus that the Barbie Twins get to decide if I'm cute enough to win.

This is all *such* a load of cat poop.

Interspecies Diplomatic Mission with the Head of the LA Humane Society

I meet the Moses of dogs, Gretchen Wyler

I think I met the prophet, the Moses of dogs. Her name is Gretchen Wyler and she is the one who is leading my furry people to the promised land. Not only was she a huge Broadway star, with the greatest legs you've ever seen (too bad she's only got two of them) but she's a big leader in the animal rights movement and she wanted to meet *me*!

Mom is a big fan of hers too and they had fun talking about animal rights, show biz, and of course, men.

Gretchen: "Oh, I had a *great* time when I was on Broadway. I knew them *all*! Some of them are still alive, so I can't write *that* book yet!"

Mom: "Ooh! Tell me about some of the good dead ones!"

Gretchen: "Charlton Heston."

Mom: "Charlton Heston? He's alive, isn't he?"

Gretchen: "Well, he's half dead anyway."

Mom: (laughing) "You were with Ben-Hur and he was *bad*?"

Gretchen: "Awful."

Maybe she thought he was dead because he seemed that way in bed. His acting career's been dead for a while. And he was kind of dead as an actor in *Soylent Green*. I always see him on TV, pumping a hunting rifle in the air at those NRA conventions. What's *wrong* with him, encouraging people to shoot and kill animals for fun?

Mom: "But boy, was he gorgeous."

Gretchen: "*Gorgeous*."

Then the most embarrassing thing happened. Gretchen, the Martin Luther King Jr. of dogs, was eating her lunch at her desk and I farted. By accident, I detonated an atomic fart missile. This was no ordinary fart, but a stinking cloud of noxious gas that could melt wallpaper and fog up windows. She was so nice about it. She didn't get mad; she kept right on eating her tofu salad. I wanted to apologize but I was too star-struck.

Mom: "Oh, no. I hate to tell you this in the middle of your lunch, but Jinky just passed an ill wind. He's very sorry."

Gretchen: "At least it wasn't you, Carole."

While my bad gas was clearing, Gretchen changed the subject and told me about a bill that the Humane Society is trying to pass for elephants in California. They don't want humans to be allowed to use bull hooks or baseball bats to beat up elephants anymore. I told Gretchen about when I met a gorgeous elephant girl at a movie studio a couple of years ago. (I wanted to hump her but she was too tall.) The elephant was sad. She told me she had been kidnapped from her family and friends and sold to a circus. Circuses are horror shows for the animals and anybody who's been *backstage* knows it.

It's a good thing that Gretchen "Moses" Wyler the dog prophet is retiring from the Humane Society and moving out of that office in a few weeks, because I think I gassed the office so bad, it's no longer possible to work in there.

Losers and Saboteurs

Photo by Maximilian Canepa

Losers! That's what we are.

The "Nuts for Mutts" Dog Show was a disaster—a catas-
trophe. Mom really wanted me to win and I placed in the
top ten for Terrier Mixes but in the end, I was a total

loser. It ought to have been called the "Mutts with No Nuts" show because none of the dogs had any balls.

It started out badly because we had to force Dad to get up early and Dad hates to get up at all. Then we had to drive all the way out to Woodland Hills with only one cup of coffee in Dad's tank and he needs at least two double espressos in order to avoid an accident on the freeway.

Mom was an anxious wreck about me placing in the top three. What a pain. I don't give rat's poop hole what these neurotic Hollywood dog show crazies think about me. I was just doing it because the money it took to register me in the contest goes to New Leash on Life, a rescue organization that helps my old cell mates. I endured the humiliation for the cause.

On the way out to "No Nuts for Mutts," Finley spread out on the floor of the Z4 like a blob, and Mom gelled my head fur so that it looked spikey on top and lectured me about my manners. But it was no use. As soon as I got in the ring with the other terriers, I knew it was over. The judge got too close to me with what looked like a weapon (turns out it was only a microphone), and I kind of tried to bite her.

Jillian Barberie, the hottie from *Good Day LA*, said, "I *like that* dog!" She's the only one of the judges who understood that I was having a flashback from my former owners who used to beat me. Two other celebrity judges, Nicole Sullivan and Richard Pryor's widow, Jennifer Lee Pryor, gasped in horror.

Then the announcer walked up to me with an even bigger microphone and I swear, he looked like he was going to hit me over the head with it. First, I growled my most ferocious growl into it. The crowd went wild. Then he stepped forward, menacing me, and I had no choice.

I bit the microphone right out of his hand. He jumped back. The crowd roared. It was like a scene out of *Gladiator*.

Mom: (screaming) "No, Jinky! No! Don't bite the judges! We'll get sued! We won't just lose this show, we'll lose the *house*!"

And then, a plain, ordinary terrier crawled up to the judge and licked her. He sat down, put his paws up on her, and gave her a long, wet kiss from her neck to her forehead. The crowd sighed, "Aw!" The woman who was showing him said he was a service dog and that she, the owner, had a neurological disability. That was it.

Dad: "Well, that's it. It's over. We know who is going to win *this* show. The kiss-ass."

Now I know how Mom feels when she goes on auditions.

I think that just living in this crazy city is enough to acquire a neurological disability, and I'm sure Mom could have faked one anyway. Dad did that when he was in the army. He faked insanity to get out of Germany (not during WWII, but during Vietnam, but that's another story).

That's Hollywood. It's not about who's the best terrier. The guy who's honest and real is the loser and the guy who wins is a suck-up.

Sung to "We are the Champions":

> We are the losers
> *We* are the losers
> . . . of the world.

Water Wonderful World

I like to sit here in the Jacuzzi and think sometimes. I think about why people drive themselves and
everybody else crazy with worry. They worry that it's
the end of the world all the time. And yet, they have
so much more time than me. I've only got a good ten
summers left in my life and then it's over but I'm
going to enjoy every minute of it now. I wish I could
teach Mom and Dad some of the things I learned at the
pound—that the worst thing in the world can somehow
turn out to be the best thing in the world.

If I didn't get thrown onto death row in San Pedro,
then I never would have met the people from Chihuahua Rescue, who then got me to the greatest place on
earth, here. See?

Just when you think you're going to get the noose
around your neck, your whole life can turn around.
Just because a couple of decent people decided to do
what's right. Because of them, I can relax here in my
Jacuzzi and watch the bubbles come up to the surface
like ideas.

Yup, I can sit here in the wet, cozy hot water and
feel the sun on my face. I can smell the delicious
stuff Mom's cooking upstairs in the kitchen. I can
hear Stupid Kitty clawing the couch. I can see Finley
chasing rats in the ivy and I can see Dad passed out
with a book in the hammock. I can sit here and know
my whole pack is safe.

I figure if I wag my tail in here, it causes the
water to move around and the ripple goes over into

the pool, where *that* water gets moved around. Then a bee, drowning on the ripple, gets moved closer to the edge of the pool and saved, and then the bee can dry his wings and he's able to go and feed his kids, who grow up and pollinate the whole place so birds will come and hang out and sing—all because I wagged my tail in the Jacuzzi.

All these things are connected. Maybe if I wag my tail enough, I can make the world right.

A NOTE FROM THE AUTHOR

You might think Jinky's story is fluffy and cute but what compelled me to write it is an ongoing tragedy. I feel as though Jinky is speaking through me, trying to let you know that millions of companion animals are killed in the shelter system, on the streets, and in laboratories every year.

The situation is urgent.

Right now, millions of dogs and cats are abandoned, alone, and afraid. They did nothing to deserve their fate, and all they want is someone to love who will treat them with kindness. These defenseless animals are going to die this year and every year unless we take action.

What can we do? *A lot.*

- Next time, don't buy a pet. *Adopt.* Buying a pet only perpetuates an industry that creates millions of surplus pets for profit.
- Spay or neuter your companion animal.
- Give to rescue organizations.
- Volunteer at your local rescue organization.
- Get involved in the political process and make sure your representatives in government are aware that their constituents (you) want them to work on legislation that abolishes animal cruelty.
- Report animal cruelty to the police. It's a crime.

If you want a specific breed, you can go to Google.com and type in the name of the breed followed by the word "rescue." Or you can go to Petfinder.com and do a search by breed. You can find anything you want because, guess what? Purebred or mutt, someone else's "garbage" might end up being your best friend.

Personally, I think mutts are the cutest, the smartest, and the healthiest, but I love my Finley and she's a pure Cairn terrier who is "show quality." Being a show-quality Cairn didn't save her from abandonment, though. Somebody spent over $1,000 to buy her as a puppy and then they dumped her.

Don't listen to all that baloney about not knowing what you're getting when you don't buy a puppy. Hogwash. It's the same as with people. Did you choose all your friends when they were infants? Must you know someone as a baby to love him today? No, you either click or you don't. When you go to meet a potential four-legged friend at a shelter, you see if you click and then everything else can be worked out with a little time, patience, and understanding. After a few weeks, you will bond like Krazy Glue.

Remember that puppies become dogs and kittens become cats in a couple of months.

Many of the dogs and cats in the shelters are there because people bought an expensive purebred two-month-old and ended up not liking what they got. That animal might be perfect for you!

Imagine if something happened to you and your beloved dog or cat was alone in the world. What would happen to him? Unless you're one of the few who have made arrangements, he'd end up in a shelter, dependent on the kindness of strangers. What if he wasn't a puppy anymore? Does that make him less valuable? I think we get better as we get older—we get smarter and deeper. I might not command the same salary on the market as an actress anymore and I'm too old to enter a beauty contest but I'm a better companion now. The same goes for pets.

For those who want to show their children "the miracle of life" by breeding their own dog, I say the other miracle, the end *result* of "the miracle of life," is the miracle of *death*. A more valuable lesson about animals is the one about responsible pet guardian-ship and about what happens to all those puppies and kittens when they get dumped. It's a miracle if they survive.

If you want a pet but think you don't have time for one, re-member that the one who is out of time is the one in the cage at the pound, with hours to live before being put down. He will be happy just to have a loving home. You can always get somebody to walk your dog while you are at work.

And if you think you have no space if you live in an apart-ment, remember that many dogs live out their sad lives chained to a fence in a big yard. A pet is happy in a studio apartment if you love him and exercise him every day. Some very big people live in tiny apartments. Go for a nice long walk—it'll be good for both of you.

If you've already rescued an animal, then you and I are on the same page. We are part of a surging tide of change, saving one animal at a time and enriching our lives by the meaningful connection we make with others who rescue. We are a community and we are never alone.

Jinky gave me more than I ever imagined. He's taught me about joy, spontaneity, compassion, and commitment. He makes me laugh, he makes me cry, and he makes me happy. He taught me the secret to a satisfying life—enthusiasm! And to think that somebody beat him up and dumped him makes me really mad. He was thrown out like garbage, left to die at the pound.

Look at him now.

Jinky is the underdog—he's also the everydog. There are millions of Jinkys shivering in cages right now waiting for your love.

Go *get* one.